MW01048853

HELP!
I'M IN THE BAND!

Deb —
Thanks for your work
on this book & being a
good friend.

HELP!
I'M IN THE BAND!

Gregory L. Metcalf

ᴘ

METCOR PUBLICATIONS

Lake Stevens

Copyright © 2011 by Gregory L. Metcalf

All rights reserved.

PUBLISHED BY METCOR PUBLICATIONS
PO Box 1249
Lake Stevens, WA 98258

Designed by Gregory L. Metcalf

Printed in the United States of America

ISBN-10: 0615586228
ISBN-13: 978-0-615-58622-9

To my son,
   John Gregory Metcalf

CONTENTS

Contents

ACKNOWLEDGMENTS

I owe much inspiration to my son, John. He would find humor in my various stories of the bands that I taught and the bands I was in. Being the artist and listener that he is, and the fact he is able to withstand the full onslaught of a beginning band in concert, his suggestions and support have been priceless.

I would also be remiss if I didn't include a sincere thanks to the many who helped me with proofreading and editing of this book. They have also been invaluable to me by the simple effect of an encouraging word here and there. I hope that these people will accept my sincere gratitude:
Scott Boal, Jackie Bosworth, Leanne Geary, Paul Gillespie, Sarena Hyman, John Metcalf, Mike Mines, Linda Pilcher, Linda Saint, Peg Shipley, Dave Stangland, Robin Stangland, Debbie Wade, and Gary Whitney.

THE FIELD TRIP

In most of the secondary schools of the United States you will find the school band. Lost Hollow High School has one band made up of 9th through 12th graders. This is a story about how that group, the "Lost Hollow High School Muskrat Band," took their first ever field trip.

Many years ago, in my second year as the band teacher, I was having breakfast on a Saturday morning down at Mabel's Cafe with a couple of my cronies, Cranky Cranklemeyer and Tom Brandston.

"Those eggs look pretty good, Greg," mentioned Tom, indicating my plate with his fork.

"These are pancakes, Tom," I retorted with a slightly squeamish look on my face. Mabel was not known for her culinary delights. In fact, the only things Mabel COULD cook for breakfast that looked edible were eggs. I was kicking myself for not ordering them.

"Ow!" barked Tom. "Who's kicking!"

If it was determined by looks alone, my two friends could have been the Laurel & Hardy of recent times. They seem to be such opposites. When standing, Tom with his lanky thin six-foot-two frame, towered over Cranky, who was a very stocky five-foot-nine. Tom had medium length dark hair that was almost black, whereas Cranky's hair was a reddish blonde, with some graying along the sides. Neither one sported any facial hair like my full beard.

Just then Mrs. Stubbleberg walked in to the restaurant, spotted us, and came up to our table. "Hello gentlemen," she cooed, smiling at Cranky.

"Hello, Mrs. Stubbleberg," came the unison chorus from the three of us. Mrs. Stubbleberg was the 4th grade teacher for the three of us almost twenty years ago and still had the ability to have us grovel in our seats, now that she was the principal of Lost Hollow High School. She had always liked Cranky, who was known as her "teacher's pet." I assumed it was because he always gave her an apple every day. He hated apples.

"I just heard that the High School Band Festival is going to be held in Anacortes next month," she said. "Do you think you will be taking our Muskrat Band to that event this year?"

I just realized she was looking directly at me. Seeing those historical eyes boring in on me caused me to forget everything I knew......where I was, what Mrs. Stubbleberg just asked me, my name.........

"Come, come, Greg" said Mrs. Stubbleberg, waiting. "You look like you just forgot your name!"

"It's Greg, it's Greg!" I stammered, thankful for the hint. "I, uh, hadn't thought about the band festival. I must not have gotten the paperwork," I hoped, not wanting to get involved in something that might actually cause me to have to work a little more than usual.

"Nonsense!" exclaimed Mrs. Stubbleberg, showing one of her piercing looks. "I put the application in your mailbox personally, right after I made a copy of it. I happen to be on the Board of Directors for the festival. If you've lost the application I can get you another."

"Oh. Th..Thanks." I replied morosely.

As Mrs. S. began to walk away she intoned, "I'll put the paperwork in your box again, Greg. Try not to lose it." The last sentence was said with a grin that showed teeth that were implanted from a shark and a look that bored a hole directly through my right eye, through the wall, and into the next county.

"Wow!" exclaimed Tom. "Did you see those teeth?"

"Alright, guys, you've got to help me figure out a way to get out of this festival," I choked. I shouldn't have had that last bite of pancakes.

"Aw, it can't be that bad, Greg," mentioned Cranky.

"Bad?!" I exclaimed. "Don't you realize that this will involve a, ...a, ... I could hardly say it ..... FIELD TRIP!?" Just then I heard high-pitched, short violin notes that seemed to come out of an old Alfred Hitchcock movie. This, of course, caused me to levitate about 2 inches out of my chair.

"Why are you so jumpy?" responded Tom.

"Didn't you hear that music?" I whimpered. It came right out of that old Hitchcock mov...."

"That's the brakes on Lyle's pickup truck that just pulled up to the café," scoffed Cranky. "Besides, you are NOT going to get out of this one, Greg. Didn't you hear that Stubbs said she is on the Board of Directors of the festival?"

"Great," I said resigning myself to the inevitable.

"Now eat your eggs and lets go," said Cranky, scowling.

"These are panc... oh, never mind," I responded, gloomily, as I shoved my plate away.

When the fateful day of the field trip arrived I figured that I had prepared as much as possible for this monumental occasion.

"What's that body armor for, Mr. Olson?" enquired a nosey 9th grade trumpet player.

"All right you kids!" I barked. "I don't want to see any gouging, clawing, kicking or elbows. Make this a clean...."

"Mr. Olson, we are just getting on the bus," stated one of my more factual clarinctists.

"Well, I wish you well," said Cranky, pumping my hand. "By the way, if you don't come back can I have your guitar?"

"I am only going for the day, Cranky," I replied. The way he smiled was unnerving.

"If we don't get a move on we'll be late!" barked the bus driver, who was a little old lady who was about 110 years old.

I counted the 33 kids and had a seat in the front of the bus. "What are those blocks strapped to your shoes?" I asked.

"I can't reach the brakes without 'em!" cackled the driver.

"But, but...."

Just then the bus lurched forward and we were off. I looked out my window in a slight panic and saw Cranky, smiling, and strumming an imaginary guitar.

"We had gone about ten miles with no problems and I was beginning to relax in my seat when I heard from the last row of the bus, "99 bottles of beer on the wall..." being sung by one of the less in-tune drummers. Immediately, I leapt to my feet grabbing my emergency kit, and headed to the back of the bus. I was already prepared for this. As I reached the back of the bus I exclaimed to the drummer, "How did you get that cut on your lip?"

"What cut?" he responded.

"It's ok," I said. "I have plenty of band-aids."

"But that looks like duct taay....mmmph."

My father always taught me to be prepared.

The next hour was fairly uneventful except for the fact that the heater broke and we had to pull over for Barney Wertelmeyer, the clarinet player whose alias was *Ragweed*.

"I have to go pee really bad, Mr. Olson, and if I don't go in the next couple of minutes the bus is going to get really wet," exclaimed *Ragweed*. The thing about *Ragweed* was that he was extremely truthful. The bus screeched to a halt and *Ragweed* ran into the forest, coming back a few minutes later, scratching his legs, arms, and face.

"I think I got into some stinging nettles, Mr. Olson," came his account.

"Oh, great," I said, thinking that I didn't have any ointments.

"Mickey, do you have any your slide cream?" I asked of one of the closer trombonists.

"Sure, Mr. Olson," he replied, opening his case and handing me his jar.

By the time we were done with *Ragweed* he looked like the Pillsbury Dough Boy. "Gosh, thanks, Mr. Olson!" said *Ragweed*. "Don't mention it," I said, noticing that I could see my breath. "Is there any chance of getting some heat on this bus?" I asked of the bus driver.

"As soon as we get to Anacortes I'll have someone look at it," she said. As I looked back at the kids they were blowing into their hands and patting their arms, trying to get the circulation going."

We pulled into the Anacortes High School parking lot and all the kids were staring at the school with their mouths open. "Look," one of them exclaimed, "that building is huge!"

"And the classrooms have windows!" stated another. "They have a lawn with real grass in the front!" shouted out still another.

"Now, now, students! They are human just like the rest of us," I stated, looking doubtfully at Ragweed. "Let's get our gear and get off the bus."

As Tommy, who had the alias of *Blap*, stepped off the bus he said, "This is a small step for man......" *Blap* had never been on a field trip before.

"Shut up and get moving!" shouted Jimmy Thornbush, one of the trumpet players.

Once we were off the bus I counted 32 students and if you were paying attention earlier you know that I was one short. I got back on the bus and saw *Ragweed* crouched down behind the last seat. "What's wrong, *Ragw...* er, Barney?" I asked.

"I look like the Pillsbury Dough Boy," stated *Ragweed*.

"Nonsense," I said. "Once you have your uniform on nobody will notice anything."

"Were we supposed to bring our uniforms?" he asked.

All of a sudden I began to feel my asthma coming on. Usually, *Ragweed* had to play his clarinet to produce that effect in me. "You forgot your uniform!?" I stammered.

"I don't think Mickey brought his, either," whimpered *Ragweed*.

As I got off the bus and was wondering if this world would be ok with one less clarinet player, I asked, "How many of you forgot your uniforms?"

Four hands went up. "Oh, great," I exclaimed. "Now what do we do?"

"I know," said *Blap*. Someone can wear my black shirt and you can make a sash out of your grey duct tape." Our uniform had a black top with a grey sash placed diagonally on the front.

"That's got to be one of the most ridiculous ideas I have ever heard," I said, reaching for my duct tape. "Who wants to wear *Blap*'s shirt?" Instantly, 32 bodies backed away, leaving *Blap* in the middle of a ring of band students. *Blap* was not known for taking showers and washing his clothes unless some special occasion was coming.

"Come on, guys," said *Blap*, "I took a shower and washed all my clothes last night getting ready for this festival."

"Oh, all right," *Ragweed* said, disgustedly. "I'll wear it." I guess the fact that *Blap* wears a double extra large and *Ragweed* wears a small didn't dawn on *him*.

"Well, if you won't be needing me for a while," said the bus driver, "I'll go try to find someone to fix that heater and get some lunch." After making sure everyone had everything they needed off the bus we said goodbye to the bus driver and started getting everyone decked out in some form of a uniform, with four of the students wearing duct tape sashes. We walked into the school and approached the registration table where I proclaimed, "We are from Lost Hollow High School."

"Where is the rest of your band?" asked a woman whose nose was slightly higher than every other nose in the room. She could have been the double for the evil queen in a recent movie I had just seen.

"This is it!" I smiled.

"Oh," she said. I had never known how condescending the word "Oh" could be until that moment. "Those are interesting uniforms," she said sweetly, staring at the duct-taped musicians. "You need to head over to the warm-up room because you perform in 30 minutes," she said. "Our guide will lead you."

As soon as we entered the warm-up room I instructed our students to warm-up. They immediately started jumping up and down, patting their arms and blowing into their hands. "I meant on your instruments!!" I yelled.

Just then Jimmy shouted, "I think I left my trumpet on the bus!" Without hesitation I barked, "Quick! Catch the bus before it leaves!"

"And see if my music is there, too!" yelled *Blap*, as Jimmy took off on a run. The look I gave the shrinking *Blap* was about .45 caliber.

"What do we do now?" queried *Ragweed*.

"Keep warming up!" I demanded. After a couple of minutes of cacophony I got Priscilla's attention and motioned for her to come up front. Priscilla was the president of the band, which meant she got to direct the band for various warm-ups and pep band events. "Priscilla," I said, "I want you to run the band through the first song."

"Ok, Mr. Olson," she chimed. As Priscilla started leading I began thinking about what to do about the missing music and trumpet player, noticing the clock ominously showing only 10 minutes left for our warm-up time. The continued torrent of noises brought me out of my contemplation. "Priscilla!" I yelled over the tumult, "I wanted you to run through the first number!"

"That's what we're playing, now, Mr. Olson," came the reply.

That caused me to think of what kind of scores were given at these events and if we were about to set a new record for the lowest one ever given.

"Are you still cold, Mr. Olson?" asked the ever-inquisitive *Ragweed*. "You are shuddering."

Just then a voice behind me said, "You have to head to the stage, now." I turned and saw our guide holding her hands over her ears.

As we shuffled to the stage I was wondering if it was too late for prayer. *Ragweed* interrupted my thoughts with, "Do you think I could actually use a reed this time, Mr. Olson?" Because of the unusual nature of *Ragweed's* tone I had decided a long time ago to have him hum through his clarinet instead of using an actual reed. Whenever he played his clarinet with a reed, *Ragweed* had the ability of putting people into a trance-like state that we had coined the Daymare (which is not much different than a nightmare). The result would be grotesque facial expressions, wide eyes, and fainting. For some reason I was affected in a different way, with wheezing and palpitations.

"Absolutely NOT!" I stammered, wondering if there was a side door through which I could casually slip out.

As the kids organized themselves on the stage I looked out past the stage lights and saw six eyes peering at me. "What kind of beast is that?" I asked the guide, with a shudder.

"Those are the judges," glowered the guide. As the judges smiled at me I was reminded of my principal's teeth down at Mabel's.

"Could we have a few more minutes?" I asked the guide in desperation. "I am waiting for my trumpet player and…."

"I am sorry," came a cold voice behind me. It was the evil queen. For some reason I was beginning to have cravings for Turkish Delight. I guess you had to see the movie……….

"We are on a tight time schedule," she continued, "and you will have to begin your program now."

Without a trumpet player and no tuba music we began our first number. The sounds coming out of the band reminded me of the New York Philharmonic……when they are warming up. Actually, our sounds were not that good. I turned and saw the same smiles from the judges, except that now their heads were bobbing up and down, not much different than someone who is laughing uncontrollably. I am not sure what caused my next action but I leaned over to *Ragweed* and said, "Put your reed on, Barney."

"Really?" came the reply. "Now?"

"Yes, now!" I hissed.

Within seconds there came a wailing out of the band that I recognized. It was *Blap*, who had noticed *Ragweed* putting on his reed. But before *Blap* could alert the rest of the band a horrific resonance began to pierce the auditorium like a knife through soft butter. As the sound began to fill the room I turned and saw the judges with faces cast in hideous form, which was not unlike most of the faces of the audience members. In fact, my band students had stopped playing their instruments and began mimicking the look of the audience. As I reached for my inhaler, *Ragweed* was just taking a breath to begin another phrase. I instantly gave the cut sign and had my band stand up as if we just finished the performance.

At first there was no sound but then some polite applause began scattered throughout the room. I hurriedly ushered my band off the stage and to the warm up room to get our cases. As we headed outside I saw our bus pulling up.

"We got the heater fixed!" exclaimed the bus driver, smiling. "Hey, what's wrong with you? You look as if you'd seen a ghost."

"It was worse," I stated.

Then I noticed Jimmy sitting in the front seat. He was covered with mud, his clothes were in tatters, and his glasses were missing one lens. "What happened to you?" I asked.

"Well, it's a long story, Mr. Olson," began Jimmy.

"Never mind," I said, exhaustedly. "You can tell me later."

After counting the students I saw the evil queen heading out to our bus. "Quick!" I said to the bus driver. "Let's head out of here!" But I was too late because the queen had reached our bus.

"Mr. Olson! Mr. Olson!" she shouted. I have your scores here. She handed me the envelope with the sheets. As I opened it with trepidation I noticed how quiet it was on the bus with every kid staring at me. As I looked at the scores my jaw fell off my face and bounced on the floor of the bus before coming to rest in a position of shock.

"Why these scores are all in the Superior range," I stated in disbelief.

The queen said, "It seems that all memory of your performance was completely wiped out of the minds of all three judges (not to mention everyone else in the auditorium). They couldn't remember you making any mistakes so they gave you the highest score of Superior."

Instantly, a cheer rose up from the kids on the bus. On the way home there was laughter and singing.

From that day our band became somewhat town heroes and Mabel even gave me a free pancake breakfast. As I was having that breakfast down at Mabel's the next Saturday with Tom and Cranky, Tom said, "Boy, you certainly have made Mrs. Stubbleberg's good list. She has been telling everybody what a great band we have."

"I know," I said gloomily.

"Why so glum?" asked Cranky. "I would have thought you would be soaking it up!"

I replied, "Now that everyone thinks we are so great we are getting requests to have us play at the all the events around the county. That would mean more...... (I gulped)...... field trips." Instantly, there arose those high-pitched, short violin notes again, which caused me to leap out of my chair.

"I sure wish Lyle would get his brakes fixed," complained Tom.

Just then Mabel came up to the table. "In honor of our award winning band director I fixed something special for you boys," she said, proudly, as she set the plate on the table. As I reached for the cover of the dish I asked, "What's it called, Mabel?"

"It's called Turkish Delight!"

My right hand froze in mid-air as my left reached for my inhaler.

THE OFFICIAL BAND EXCUSE LIST

I am sure that at one time or another you have come across a purported excuse list for school, band, or whatever. Fortunately, I have saved you from some cheap imitation for this IS the actual "OFFICIAL EXCUSE LIST FOR BAND." Take a moment and see how many of these you can memorize because if your band teacher is anything like me then you know that we hate to waste time. So if you come to class late, without your music, and your instrument fell off the roof of your car because you forgot that you put it up there…then just say, "Mr. (Ms.) _____, excuses number 5, 25 and 185." See? In just 5 seconds or less you have said everything a 6-minute explanation would barely touch on!

Here's the list:
1. I forgot. (Whew, only two words, and you can't BELIEVE how many students fail to memorize THIS one!)
2. My dog ate it. (You may substitute cat, python, alligator, but NOT polar bear unless you live in Alaska)
3. My instrument is broken.
4. I can't play my __(instrument)_ because my dad stuck it into the wall (this one actually works!)
5. I lost my music.
6. I was late because my alarm didn't go off, honestly, really!

7. I couldn't practice because I am allergic to practicing and break out in hives.
8. My mom washed my music.
9. My mom washed my practice sheet.
10. I locked my instrument case and can't find the key.
11. My mom washed my saxophone (try this only as a last resort).
12. My mom forgot to wake me up.
13. My dad forgot to wake me up.
14. I was tardy because my trumpet got stuck in the toilet.
15. My dog chewed up my drum sticks (this could be classified as a variation on #2).
16. My locker won't open.
17. My flute got wet in the rain so I tried to dry it in the microwave oven. We plan to get another one.... oven, I mean.
18. Five aliens jumped me on the way to school, grabbed my practice sheet out of my book bag, and took off in their orange, err purple, err silver flying saucer.
19. I am tardy because I am protesting against digital clocks (analog may be inserted in the place of "digital").
20. I was busy.
21. I got stuck in the elevator.
22. I got stuck in the custodian's closet after I blew my trumpet in his ear.
23. Something is wrong with my instrument so I didn't bring it.
24. My partner has my music.
25. I was late because the bell rang earlier than it should have.
26. I fell down the stairs while practicing my marching and will get my saxophone fixed right after I see Dr. Wilson.
27. I lost my practice sheet while fighting with a kid who said you weren't the best band director in the world.
28. I can't play today because my head was hurt when my brother decided to play my crash cymbals.
29. My clarinet got stuck in my hair. My dad took it to get it fixed.... the clarinet, that is.
30. On the way home from school I saved a lady's purse from a purse-snatcher but tripped on my trombone after I threw it at him.

31. I was so busy practicing last night I forgot to write the time down on my practice sheet.
32. I can't play today because my cat has a headache.
33. I couldn't go to band yesterday because I was planning a funeral for my recently deceased goldfish.
34. I didn't turn in my practice sheet because my dog pooped on it, but I have it right here if you would like to see it?
35. I can't play my flute right now because I have a very contagious strep throat infection.
36. Billy threw my trumpet out the school bus window. Now it plays a little flat. Heh, heh.
37. I couldn't come to band yesterday because my parents forgot and locked me in my house.
38. I am tardy because I had to wait for my nails to dry.
39. My dog ate my pencil.
40. I have a hard time playing American music with my French horn.
41. My music got flushed down the toilet.
42. Practicing gets in the way of my social life.
43. I broke my glasses
44. Yesterday I drowned but now I am resusticated
45. We were caught in traffic…for the past week.
46. Someone stole my music. We are checking the pawnshops this evening.
47. Someone stole my instrument, but then returned it to my house after I left for school.
48. I didn't want to.
49. Someone stole my pencil.
50. My clock broke so I couldn't practice.
51. I didn't practice 'cause my cat had kittens and I didn't want to scare them.
52. My parents said I had to practice in the garage but there was no room in there.
53. My brother broke my instrument (after I played a loud note in his ear).
54. My dog swallowed my piccolo.
55. I can't play my tuba until I get my pet snake out of it.

56. I dreamt I practiced all night and when I woke up my embouchure muscles were too tired to practice.
57. My trumpet fell underneath the bleachers.
58. I just got braces.
59. I just got my braces tightened.
60. I won't be at the concert tomorrow night. My family is going on a ten-country tour and we just found out about it today.
61. I can't play my flute because I hyperventilate.
62. I can't play my drum because I hyperventilate.
63. I am late because I forgot to look at my watch.
64. I broke my finger - arm wrestling.
65. I can't play my trombone because I have tennis elbow.
66. We ran out of gas.
67. We had a flat tire.
68. Our radiator broke.
69. Our brakes don't work.
70. We don't have a car so we started thinking about how to get to the concert about ten minutes before it started.
71. I couldn't find my uniform.
72. The cat turned off my alarm.
73. I couldn't come to the concert because my favorite TV show was on and this was the final episode.
74. I couldn't come to the concert because my favorite TV show was on and this episode was as good as the final episode.
75. I couldn't come to school last week because we were waiting for my momma's baby to arrive.
76. I locked myself in the bathroom.
77. I sprained my finger on the remote control last night.
78. Our dog ate my mom's car keys.
79. I took my clarinet apart and couldn't figure out how to put it together. Could you do it?
80. I was so busy using my saxophone to get my dog to howl I forgot about the concert.
81. My mouthpiece is dirty so I can't play my instrument until I clean it.
82. I couldn't find any matching socks.
83. My metabolism has slowed too much and I need chocolate.

84. I was practicing so hard that I passed out and missed the concert.
85. I put on too much valve oil so now my valves play the notes too fast.
86. My part has wrong notes in it.
87. I forgot my glasses.
88. I have to slouch because of a kink in my back.
89. Brass instruments can't play that soft.
90. I was playing the wrong song.
91. I was still celebrating my birthday.
92. The bus came too soon and I missed it.
93. My son/daughter was tired so I let him/her sleep in.
94. I haven't practiced so I need you to take the song slower.
95. A pad fell out of my flute.
96. I was cleaning my instrument and my mouthpiece fell into the disposal. You can guess the rest…
97. I was suspended for playing my trumpet too loud in math class.
98. I had to give my cat a bath and I ended up in the emergency room.
99. My brother dropped my piccolo into the blender.
100. My reed is too soft.
101. My reed is too hard.
102. All of my reeds are broken and I didn't think about getting new ones until the concert started.
103. I had to finish my homework.
104. Notes that high can't be tuned.
105. My lips are chapped.
106. Our car broke down.
107. Our boat broke down.
108. My bike broke down.
109. I was running to get to the concert and when my saxophone fell out of the case and I accidentally kicked it…..
110. I was late because I have strep throat (cough, cough).
111. My mom was trying a new recipe and I got food poisoning.
112. My instrument was due for its annual cleaning so I took it in yesterday just before the concert.

113. I know our concert starts in a few minutes but would it be ok if I don't play my solo because I just had my braces tightened today.
114. I didn't buy any more clarinet reeds because I think I am allergic to them.
115. I can't stay to the end of the concert because I will be violating my parole.
116. My dad was speeding to get me to the concert but got pulled over by a policeman who cited him for driving without a drivers license and then arrested him for having 24 unpaid speeding tickets and I had to walk the rest of the way uphill and in the snow............
117. I am allergic to the snare drum.
118. My dog told me not to go to the concert.
119. My father threw my drum on top of the roof and forgot we don't have a ladder.
120. I don't have my trombone because I am having it painted orange.
121. Uncle Barrymore escaped again.
122. I broke a nail and I just couldn't have anybody see me like that, could I?
123. I was buthy getting my tongue pierthed. You know, it'th a bit harder to play flute thith way.
124. I was busy getting a tattoo. Forty-three and counting!
125. I have the farts and saved the concert by not coming.
126. I am stalling because I am thinking of an excuse.
127. My practice record fell into a shredder.
128. I missed the concert because I found out from a TV show that I have leprosy.
129. My legs fell asleep and I couldn't get out of my chair.
130. I couldn't take my trombone apart to put it in its case.
131. One of my trumpet valves is missing. Have you seen it?
132. I can't find my mouthpiece.
133. I forgot my mouthpiece.
134. I couldn't practice because we live in an apartment whose walls are mostly paper.
135. Mute? I thought the note said to buy a mutt!

136. My tuning slides are stuck and I KNOW that I greased them last year!
137. My mouthpiece got stuck so my dad took a pair of pliers……..
138. I couldn't practice because I had to write 400 times, "I will not stuff the cat in my baritone horn."
139. The bus driver won't let me take my trumpet on the bus anymore.
140. I couldn't find my flute but I think it's in my closet somewhere.
141. My arm got stuck in the loops of my French horn and my dad had to help me get it out. The horn is now in the repair shop getting it re-looped.
142. I don't like 16th notes.
143. My music stand was too low.
144. My music stand was too high.
145. My reed was too dry.
146. My reed was too wet.
147. My mouth was too dry.
148. One of clarinet keys fell off.
149. I have a screw loose…..I mean my INSTRUMENT has a screw loose!
150. I missed my note because the tympani scared me.
151. The percussion section is too loud and I can't hear my trumpet.
152. The trumpet section is too loud and I can't hear my saxophone.
153. The saxophone section is too loud and I can't hear my flute.
154. I can't play clarinet that way. I am left-handed.
155. My parents won't let me practice my drum in the living room anymore.
156. I got gum stuck in the neck pipe.
157. A fly landed on my music and I thought it was a note.
158. My music fell off of my music stand just before my solo.
159. My padsaver was stuck inside my instrument.
160. My valves were in wrong.
161. I accidentally went to 8th position on my trombone.

162. I saw snow on the ground so I didn't think there was any school.
163. I painted my case camouflage and now I can't find it.
164. My uniform is in the wash.
165. My music was folded up in my back pocket when my mom decided to do the wash..........
166. I didn't wear my uniform because a seagull flew over me and, well, do I have to tell the rest?
167. I didn't learn the fingerings because my dad told me I am tone deaf like him............
168. I was boiling my trumpet mouthpiece but starting watching this tv show and the all the water boiled out and is a black mouthpiece ok?
169. I just heard the salmon were running so I went fishing in case this was the last chance of the year and can I make up the concert?
170. I was afraid to come to school because I heard a mosquito when I opened the door. Have you heard of the West Nile virus?
171. My girlfriend punched me in the mouth for asking if she had gained weight lately.
172. I forgot my music in my locker.
173. I left my instrument in the trunk of my dad's car and I stay with my mom this week.
174. I accidentally turned off my alarm when I thought I was turning it on.
175. I didn't practice because I thought I already knew it.
176. My valve got stuck. I swear I oiled it just two months ago.
177. The wind from the vent blew my music off the stand.
178. My partner bumped my arm.
179. My gum stuck my reed closed.
180. I didn't play it because I don't like that part.
181. I can't play religious songs.
182. I can't play secular songs.
183. I stopped playing because the rest of my section stopped.
184. I didn't know you gave a cut-off. I thought you were waving for us to play louder.

185. I put my instrument on the roof of our car and forgot about it and we drove off and when we stopped it wasn't there anymore so we are having to retrace our route which will take approximately two days.

186. Our car got stuck in the snow so I tried to ski down to the concert but got stuck in the uphill section.

187. I forgot how to play the first note I learned in beginning band.

188. When I saw pp I thought that meant Pretty Powerful.

189. I was late because I woke up late because I went to bed late because I had to do something important after I did all the stuff my parents said were important after I did all the things my teacher said were important and, yeah…

190. Somehow my tambourine got stuck to my cat's tail and she went high up our maple tree and well, I won't have it for a little while….the tambourine, that is.

191. We ran out of kindling for the fireplace. We'll get more reeds tomorrow.

192. I was hoping that Santa would replace my folder of music that fell into the river but he must not have gotten my list.

193. My parents sold my drum and got me a flute instead. Can I start playing it today?

194. My mom hid my sticks in the oven and forgot about that when she started cooking dinner.

195. I laid my clarinet on a chair and my dad sat on it.

196. My dad accidentally stepped on my oboe……14 times.

197. You told us that you wanted us to be able to play it in our sleep so I tried that and accidentally rolled over on my bassoon. Is the neck-pipe thingy expensive?

198. I was playing my trumpet at the zoo near the elephant cages when there was this stampede…..

199. My clarinet is being used to prop up one corner of our dining table until a new leg can be made.

200. I decided to take this day off!

BIKERS FOR BAND

"Greg," began the principal, taking a huge breath, "there comes a time…….."

Oh, no. It's one of the "there comes a time" speeches. That usually spells impending doom … The last time I had heard that speech I was in 5th grade and had put a firecracker in Betty Johnson's desk.

I focused back in to the principal's speech, "….and that is why we don't have enough funds to do everything we would like to do."

"Am I being fired, Mrs. Stubbleberg?" I calmly asked, while I was on my knees with my hands clasped together.

"Get off your knees and sit down, Greg!" barked Mrs. Stubbleberg. "You are NOT being fired. However, we have to cancel one of your band classes and have you teach one section of Physical Education."

"But why?" I asked.

"Like I just got through saying, we don't have enough funds and, frankly, the townsfolk have not appreciated some of your latest concerts. The screeching at your last concert was unbearable!" stated Mrs. Stubbleberg.

"How was I to know that the audience would start screeching like that when they heard the beginning band?" I pleaded. "Besides, we have improved a lot, lately. Why, even yesterday the Mayor said we sounded pretty lame."

"And you think THAT'S improvement?" replied the principal.

"Last week he said we were 'deplorable'. I would think 'pretty lame' is much better than 'deplorable'.

"I am afraid the decision has already been made, Greg," she continued. "Look on the bright side, with a P.E. class you can really get yourself in shape."

"Yeah, right," I said, while pictures of myself doing push-ups and long distance running was filling my head.

"I am so glad the last day of school is tomorrow," said Cranky, with a large grin on his face.

"Yeah," I said, miserably.

"Well you're not the most chipper person I've eaten lunch with," said Cranky, taking a huge bite of his ham sandwich.

"That's because you weren't called into the principal's office this morning," I said, despondently.

In his usually supportive demeanor Cranky asked, "What did you do this time?" while taking another bite of his sandwich.

"It looks like they're cutting out one of the bands and giving me a P.E. class instead," I replied.

"That'll be great!" said Cranky, who was one of the school's Physical Education teachers. "We'll get to teach together."

"That would be fun but I'd rather teach band," I said, trying to remember the rules of basketball, baseball, volleyball, wrestling, football, and other games.

"So why are they cutting one of your band classes?" asked Cranky. "Did they actually come to one of your concerts?" he continued, laughing into his soup.

"How would you like to wear a noodle wig?" I replied, tersely.

As Cranky's laughter subsided he continued, "Honestly, why are they doing away with one of your bands? - tee hee."

"According to Mrs. Stubbleberg there isn't enough money in the budget." I said, sadly.

"Well," said Cranky, "if that's the problem then fix the problem."

The great thing about having John "Cranky" Cranklemeyer as a friend was that he was pretty amazing with some of his ideas, but not always. "Cranky, I don't think you are getting the whole gist of what I just said." I retorted. "There is not enough MONEY in the budget."

"I heard that," he said. "So, just raise some money." As I looked at Cranky stuff the last bit of sandwich in his mouth it dawned on me how simplistically and ingeniously Cranky's brain worked.

A month later, at the 4th of July Picnic, there were the usual sparklers going off, the whole-town potluck, balloons, jugglers, booths of people selling their wares, and the car show. "Hey, look!" exclaimed Cranky. Tom's showing off his '53 Studebaker again."

"Isn't that the car his wife had hauled to the junk yard last week?" I laughed.

"Yep. Tom had to pay 5 bucks to get it back," replied Cranky. "Frankly, I think they should have paid HIM to take it off their hands." Tom Brandston's upkeep on that ancient car was to wash it twice a year and leave it in his front yard, much to his wife's annoyance.

"Hey, Tom!" I yelled. "Do you want to help Cranky and me set up the gazebo for the performance?"

"Sure, as soon as I find someone to watch my car," he said.

"Are you afraid the junkyard guys are going to come by and steal it?" I laughed.

Tom's cold, icy stare went right through me. "Let's get going," I said. "I think it's getting pretty cold out here."

"Cold?" said Cranky. "It's 83 degrees.

When we got to the bandstand there was Sven Lindstrom, leaning on a broom. "Vell, I got it all svept and I brought town t'ose chairs and moosic stands like yoo asked," he said. "As soon as I get t'ose bandstand lights vorking ve'll be all set to go."

"Thanks, Sven. Here's the five lottery tickets I promised," I said.

"T'anks, Greg," said Sven. "Maybe I'll vin da fife pounds of Svedish meatballs like last year!"

"Do you think this is going to work, Cranky? I asked. "I've never tried to raise money with a concert before."

"Of course it'll work," replied Cranky. "The people of this town don't want to see our band program bite the dust."

"But it's not as though the kids have had much time to rehearse this last month," I rebutted, anxiously.

When the potluck was nearly over, Mayor Jon Eriksson came up to the bandstand to say a few words. "I'd like to say a few words," he began. "When I was a boy….."

"Mayor," whispered Cranky, pulling on his sleeve. "We have 3 bands playing this year. You're only going to have enough time to build up the fundraiser." Mayor Eriksson spent the next 15 minutes talking about the need for children's education, what music does for a child, and starving people in Haiti. I'm not sure why that last bit was in there but it had the desired effect. Tears were filling the ladies eyes and men were reaching for their wallets. The mayor could certainly deliver a speech!

When the mayor was done, the beginning band kids started putting their instruments together. "Are you sure you want your beginning group to play?" asked Tom, nervously eyeing the drummers.

"It was decided (mostly by Cranky) that ALL of the bands should play, even the beginning band, Tom," I explained. "Cranky seems to think the youngsters will be able to tug at the audience's heartstrings." As they started warming up there were apprehensive looks from the people sitting at the picnic tables and lawn chairs.

"Heart attacks might be more accurate," said Tom, under his breath.

"Wow!" stated Cranky. "The sound of the band hasn't improved very much, lately. They sound like a bunch of motorcycles!"

I was conscious of how true Cranky's statement was when I noticed a bunch of dust from the other end of town approaching fairly quickly. The motorcycle sound was getting louder, too. "That's not my band, Cranky," I said. "That sound is coming from THEM." I was pointing down Main Street as I counted about 50 bikes coming towards our park. As they pulled in, Tom exclaimed, "Those guys look pretty rough!"

"I don't know," I said. "Some of those tattoos look pretty nice to me. See that skull and crossed bones? I think the skull is smiling."

The leader was making his way towards the bandstand. I assumed that he was the leader because he looked as though he was 8 feet tall and fire came out of his nose when he breathed.

"This guy looks pretty mean and strong," said Tom.

"Big arms aren't always a sign of muscle," I whispered to Tom. At that moment the leader-guy grabbed one of the music stands, bent it in half, and used it to scratch his back.

"Where's the food?" he asked. At least, I thought that's what he asked. It sounded more like the growling of a grizzly bear who hadn't eaten since hibernation. Not wanting to become his next meal I pointed to the set of picnic tables where people were finishing their dinners. "Th..The food is over th..there," I stammered. "But most of it is gone by now."

"Then I think somebody needs to cook some more. My boys are hungry!" came the reply from "grizzly-man." As he was grunt...er, talking, his 'boys' started perusing the picnic tables, grabbing food from mothers, little old men and young children.

"Hey!" said Cranky. "Tell your boys to stop that!" As "grizzly-man" spun around it dawned on me that standing this close to him probably was not a good thing. As my feet left the ground I noticed he was using only one hand on the front of my shirt to raise me up. Tom was right about the strong part and I was beginning to realize the truth about the mean part, too.

"You got a problem, bud?" "grizzly-man" growled.

"No problem!" I squeaked. "Those kids would probably get fat eating all that good food."

As "grizzly-man" dropped me onto the bass drum he said, "Hey, you guys have a band! Let's hear it!"

"But it's just our begin….." I started.

"Play!!" growled "grizzly-man."

"OK, kids," I said nervously to a bunch of wide-eyed sixth graders, "get into your seats."

As the wide-eyed kids got into place, "grizzly-man" barked at his mates, "Hey, guys, we get to hear some live music. Gather 'round!" His men started meandering towards the bandstand, most of them holding balloons from the balloon man, who could be seen up in the sycamore tree.

Again, "grizzly-man" said, "Play!"

As I gave a downbeat, I waited for the inevitable roar from "grizzly-man." But, except for the roar from the beginning band, nothing else was heard. I turned to see all of "grizzly-man's" 'boys' stand there with their mouths hanging open and the beautiful release of about a hundred balloons filling the sky. As the band played on, hands started going to ears and the bikers began falling to their knees and swaying.

"Make them stop!" yelled the "grizzly-man", who was on his knees in front of the bandstand, his hands placed on both sides of his head.

I shouted over the cacophony of sounds, "We have to play until we make enough money for the band!"

"What!" shouted the unbelieving "grizzly-man."

"This is a fundraiser!" I replied. "We have to play until we raise money for the band."

As the bikers began rolling on the ground the band started in on the "1812 Overture" by Tchaikovsky, which was the drummers' favorite song. This is where they got to boom on the bass drum, emulating the cannons of the war. They were good at that.

"Please, please!" begged the "grizzly-man", who was looking a lot more sheep-like while on his knees with his hands clasped together.

"We haven't made enough money, yet!" I yelled. The truth was we hadn't made ANY money so far.

"Money! Money!" I heard "grizzly-man" yell to his troupes as I saw him pass between his men collecting a lot of green paper. He delivered money to Tom and Cranky and went back for more. Tom and Cranky started counting the bills. As "grizzly-man" delivered the rest to Tom and Cranky he said, "Please, is it enough?"

After a moment Cranky said, "This is only half of what we need." Meanwhile, some of "grizzly-man's" men were racing to their bikes.

Cranky said, "Your band is beginning to sound like motorcycles, again, Greg!"

And again I replied, "I don't think it's my band," indicating with my baton the leaving bikers." When the drummers saw my baton point they gave a huge crash on the bass drum, snare drums, and cymbals.

"Yow!" yelled "grizzly-man's" men.

I gave another baton cue, which caused another crash from the smiling percussionists. This last crash caused the rest of "grizzly-man's" gang to run for their bikes. Crash! Crash!

"Grizzly-man" yelled, "Wait for me!" as he raced to his own wheels. As the song ended, the dust at the other end of town could be seen dying away.

All of a sudden there was spontaneous applause and cheering as I turned around and saw all of the towns-people standing, whistling and applauding. I had the open-mouthed kids stand to accept their applause. Eventually the look of shock on their faces was replaced by smiles. They had just received a standing ovation, which had never occurred before in Lost Hollow, according to anyone's recollection.

Mayor Eriksson came up to the bandstand and began pumping my hand while the local newspaperman took our picture. The mayor said to me, "My boy, we are going to make this an annual event!"

"Well, your honor," I replied, "we didn't make enough money to keep this band."

As the mayor turned to see the smiling children and the drummers with their sticks in the air he turned to the microphone, "How many of you towns-folk are willing to put up the rest of the money for this band?" A unanimous cheer went up from the audience.

The mayor replied with, "I hereby decree that our town will put up the funds for this band to continue!" Another cheer went up.

Next Saturday morning, down at Mabel's café, I was enjoying steak and eggs when Cranky said, "Well, that had to be about the most exciting concert I have ever been to!"

"We actually weren't even done with all of our songs but Mayor Eriksson said that was the best place stop. He said something about diminishing returns," I commented.

"So, what are you going to do for the rest of the summer?" Cranky asked.

"Fishing," I responded. "How 'bout you?"

Cranky said, "I'm still coaching Little League and the mayor wants me to be on his finance committee."

"What about you?" I asked, nodding at Tom while devouring another fork-full of eggs.

"Well, I sold my Studebaker," said Tom. Cranky and I both looked at each other.

"You did?" asked Cranky.

"Yep. The wife said it had to go."

"What did you do with the money?" I inquired.

Through a mouthful of hashbrowns Tom replied, "Bought a motorcycle."

Cranky and I just stared at Tom.

MUSKRATS

Some school mascots are chosen because of their noble qualities. These might be eagles, patriots, falcons, lions, bears, and such. Some school mascots inspire courage, tenacity, strength, intelligence, or power. Ours does none of these things. We are the Muskrats.

Some people, when hearing the name Lost Hollow Muskrats, wonder about our mascot and sometimes about our sanity. There is a very logical reason for our choice of mascot. Lost Hollow owes an allegiance to the muskrat, and to one muskrat in particular. It was long ago, when I was in 4th grade, that the people of Lost Hollow decided to register our little high school with the US government in order to get some of those federal dollars. On the form it asked what our mascot was. We didn't have one so the town counsel got together to deliberate concerning this mascot. It was during these deliberations that a special event took place.

"Did you hear that we have a new superintendent?" Tommy Brandston asked, through a huge wad of bubblegum.

"What's a superindunt?" I asked, chewing on an equally large wad myself. We were enjoying a lazy August afternoon practicing catch at the local baseball diamond.

"Superintendent," said Tommy. "It's the guy in charge of the whole school system. I heard he's comin' all the way from Florida."

"Where's Florida?" I asked.

"I think it's in South America," said Tommy. "They have palm trees and everything."

"Wow. This super….super..er, person must have done something pretty bad to escape to here." I exclaimed.

"Naw, I think he has a PhD or something," interjected John "Cranky" Cranklemeyer, who played catcher for our team.

"Is P-H-D one of those tropical diseases?" I asked. "I haven't had all of my shots, yet."

Cranky blurted, "PhD is not a disease!"

I blew a size 2 bubble and conjectured, "You sure know a bunch of strange words, Cranky."

"Well if you would do your homework like you're supposed to, you would know 'em, too," replied Cranky. "It means he's a doctor or something."

"Ya mean someone who fixes people is gonna run our school?" asked Tommy.

"Well, maybe our school needs some fixing," Cranky replied.

"I'll say, said Tommy, "'specially when our students can't even say superintendent!" This, of course, caused a ball to be sent directly at Tommy's nose, which, fortunately, moved deftly out of the way.

"Hey you guys," I said. "I'll bet you don't know what the word 'deftly' means."

On the first day of school in September we had an all-school assembly in which all the usual speeches were presented. It was at this assembly that the new superintendent was introduced. He was a scrawny little man that looked like he had been starving in South America or something. No wonder he wanted to come here. He made up for his diminished size by using the largest words I had ever heard. As I looked around the room the kids were all looking at each other in total confusion about what he was saying. Even the teachers were looking a little bewildered. However, Mr. Crabtree the principal was smiling and nodding every time the superintendent paused for a breath.

"What language is he speaking?" I whispered to Tommy.

"I dunno," Tommy whispered back. "I think it's South American."

After half an hour the superintendent stopped speaking. There was complete silence. I think people didn't understand that his speech had ended.

"Let's hear it for Dr. Littleton!" exclaimed Mr. Crabtree as he jumped up to the microphone, with a slightly embarrassed expression. Polite applause began to fill the auditorium. As we headed to our classrooms I asked Cranky, "Did you understand anything Dr. Littleton said?"

"Of course I did," said Cranky, his nose in the air. "He just said that we only have to go to school 3 days per month and two of those days are to be spent partying!"

I am not sure how Cranky tripped going into our classroom, knocking the books out of Mrs. Stubbleberg's hands but the laughter it created was a moment to remember. "As soon as you are done laughing, Greg Olson," she said, burning her eyes into me like laser beams, "you can help John pick up my books." The way Cranky was looking at me with that shark-toothed smile I was glad that Mrs. Stubbleberg was standing right next to us. As we headed to our seats Cranky whispered, "See you at recess." He was still smiling like a shark. Somehow the tripping event didn't strike me as funny anymore.

"Class," started Mrs. Stubbleberg, "if you heard Dr. Littleton today, you know that Lost Hollow School District is in for some changes." This sounded a little disconcerting even if I didn't know what the word 'disconcerting' meant.

"Dr. Littleton believes that time away from studies causes students to forget what they have learned, creates a lack of focus and makes it hard for students to pay attention."

One of the hands went up. "What did you just say, Mrs. Stubbleberg?"

"For that reason," continued Mrs. Stubbleberg, slightly scowling, "Dr. Littleton has proposed that we only take one week off for Christmas instead of two, that we go to school the Friday after Thanksgiving, and that we not take a day off for Lumberjack Day."

During Mrs. Stubbleberg's address the kids sat in open-mouthed silence but when she said, "..not take a day off for Lumberjack Day.." the uproar was spontaneous. Lumberjack Day was not only the signal of the end of Fall, but it honored the people most involved with Lost Hollow's chief industry: logging. Lumberjack Day was filled with a carnival, games, and events, not to mention all the food and Mrs. Lindstrom's deep fried Rosettes.

"Now, now, children," Mrs. Stubbleberg soothed. "The school board hasn't decided to do that yet. They will be deliberating Dr. Littleton's proposals at the same meeting at which they are discussing the new mascot for the high school."

"When is that meeting, Mrs. Stubbleberg?" I asked in trepidation. "And can you tell me what 'trepidation' means?"

"That meeting will be Monday, one week from today, Greg."

The rest of the first day of school was carried out in relative gloom. Most of the teachers must have given the same talk in their classes because it seemed like the whole school was despondent. During recess Cranky even forgot, thankfully, about that little tripping incident in Mrs. Stubbleberg's room.

"This is the worst news I've heard since Tommy's hamster was run over by the mail-truck," said a depressed Cranky.

"I know," I responded in discouragement. "Tommy didn't eat dessert for three days!"

As Tommy came up to us we walked by Sven Lindstrom, the janitor, sweeping the back steps to the school. "Hi boys," he chimed. "Vy da glum looks?"

"Didn't ya hear about the canceled vacations?" Tommy said in a voice almost as miserable as when he lost his hamster.

"Yah, dat's right," came his response. "Ve had a meeting about dat yoost t'is morning. It seems like t'is noo superintendent doesn't beleef in any fun in life. Dat's a doggone shame iff ya ask me."

"I wish this superintendent would go back to South America where he came from," said Tommy.

"Rats, this is hard to take," said Cranky. We walked home in silence, if you could call Cranky's scuffling, silence.

The next day Lost Hollow Elementary School, Middle School, and High School all looked like a funeral procession as the kids headed to their first period classes. As Tommy, Cranky and I went down the main hall we noticed Sven Lindstrom looking at a package. "Hi, Sven," Cranky said. "What are you doing?"

"I am yoost tryin' ta read t'ese directions," said Sven.

"I'll help," said Tommy, who took the package from Sven. After a few seconds Tommy exclaimed, "This is a package of rat poison! Do we have rats here?"

"Vell, da noo superintendent t'ought he saw one and he's terribly scared off 'em. I t'ink he yoost saw a mouse."

"Did you just say he is scared of rats, Sven?" I asked.

"Yah, he tolt me he is so terrified dat he can't go back into a room dat a rat hass bin in!"

"Great," I exclaimed.

"Vhat?" asked Sven.

"Nothing, Sven. I just got an idea." Sometimes ideas come into my mind for which I feel extremely guilty.

"You sure have a guilty look on your face," Tommy said, as we continued to class.

Cranky asked, "Why did you say 'great?' "

"Don't you see? If we can scare this super...super..."

"Superintendent!" barked Tommy.

"Yeah, right," I said. "If we can scare him enough maybe he will leave and never come back!"

"And just how are we going to do that?" asked Cranky.

"We need to get the super-guy to think we are infested with rats," I replied. "I have a plan beginning to form!"

"Well, Sven, did you get that rat poison in place?" asked Dr. Littleton.

"Yah," said Sven. "I yoost hope it's enough for bote off 'em."

"Did you say both? Is there more than one?" asked the superintendent nervously.

"Vell, da tracks outside yer vindow are different sizes so I figured t'ere are more t'an one."

"Go buy some more poison!" shouted the superintendent.

"Yah, sure," said Sven. "Right away." As Sven left the room he noticed the superintendent looking nervously at the window.

Later on that day, as Dr. Littleton was walking to his car he noticed three young boys walking towards him engrossed in conversation. One boy in particular was very animated as though he were measuring something with his hands. "Yeah, the rat was this big!" he said, showing about a two and a half foot expanse between his hands. "And it was the baby!"

"What about all of those other rats?" asked another boy. "Did they ever catch them?"

"I think they got a lot of them. But they didn't get T-Rex!" the third boy stated.

"T-Rex?" said another. "Why do they call it T-Rex?"

"Because it is soooo big and has really looong teeth!" exclaimed the third boy.

"Hey you kids," interrupted Dr. Littleton, "where are these rats?"

"Oh, hello," I said. "Aren't you the new super.... super.... Dr. Littleton?"

"Yes, yes, but tell me about these rats!" blurted Dr. Littleton.

"It's probably nothing to worry about but they found a nest of 'em right underneath this office building," I stated casually, gesturing at the building Dr. Littleton had just left.

"Why, that's where my office is!" spouted the superintendent.

"I am sure they'll clear them out pretty quick," said Cranky, "except for T-Rex. He is pretty sly. He ALWAYS gets away."

"Well, we have to get home to do our homework," I said, conscientiously.

On the way home I asked Tommy, "Does Billy still have that pet rat of his?"

"I think so," said Tommy, "but if you're thinking what I'm thinking he's not going to let you take him to the superintendent's office!"

"I know, but he wouldn't mind taking him for a little fresh air in his cage, would he?" I asked, with a smile that might have gone well with a slightly crooked halo.

Wednesday was show-and-tell day in Mrs. Stubbleberg's class. Everyone was bringing something or giving a short talk about what happened during the summer. Tommy brought pictures of his dead hamster , which caused two girls to run out of the room. They looked a little green. Cranky brought his catcher's mask and demonstrated how to "block the plate." Unfortunately, during his demonstration, he ended up knocking over the plant on Mrs. Stubbleberg's desk. This, of course, started another fit of laughter.

"When you are finished laughing, Greg, come up front and give your presentation!" exclaimed Mrs. Stubbleberg. Of course, I brought my "Skipping Stones" set. These were probably the finest collection of pond-skipping stones you could find in the county. "Oohs" and "Aahs" were exclaimed by all the boys in the room.

Finally, it was Billy's turn. Billy brought a cage to the front of the room and in that cage was Annabelle, Billy's new rat. Annabelle looked like she was ready to have babies. "How nice," remarked Mrs. Stubbleberg, apprehensively.

After show-and-tell it was time for recess. After some coaxing from me, Billy decided to take Annabelle outside for some fresh air.

"Why are we going this way?" asked Billy. "This is the long way to the field."

"I just thought we should show Annabelle around our school," I replied. Billy seemed to like my concern for Annabelle.

As we rounded the corner of the building we found ourselves right under the superintendent's window. "Billy, I forgot my baseball glove in Mrs. Stubbleberg's room," I said. "Since you are so fast could you run back and get it for me? I'll give you a piece of bubblegum if you do."

"Sure!" exclaimed Billy. "Uh, could you hold Annabelle for me?"

"Well, ok, just this once," I remarked.

When Billy was out of sight I said in a loud voice, "I'm sure glad we caught this RAT!"

After a moment the superintendent's window was flung open. "Whe....where did you get THAT?" came the apprehensive interrogation from the window.

"I got this right here!" came the truthful reply. "This is the momma but I don't know where the daddy is," came another truthful comment.

"Do you think the daddy is "T-Rex"?" asked Tommy.

"I don't know," said Cranky, "but I wouldn't want to be around when he finds his mate has been captured!"

"Get that thing out of here!" shouted the superintendent.

"Right away, sir!" I exclaimed, and quickly headed out to the field while noticing the superintendent's sweating forehead.

Now something happened which was not in my plans and was unknown to everyone in Lost Hollow. The following is an account of what occurred to the best of my reckoning.

This time of year would sometimes bring some big rainstorms to the Northwest. One such storm had occurred about a week ago causing the local river to flood, which then caused part of the bank of the river to collapse. That section of bank happened to be the home of a large muskrat. When such an occurrence happens to a muskrat, it does what muskrats have been doing for countless years. It just starts building a new home, which can be a tunnel in a riverbank or a lodge much like a beaver's home. This particular muskrat, however, had pups to take care of so an immediate shelter had to be found. Of course, there is no better shelter than the basement of some nearby building. So, this particular muskrat was able to get into the basement of the closest building by gnawing a hole into some rotted cellar door wood.

From his window the superintendent was noticing that the nearby Stagomish River was starting to recede from its flood stage. Just then he heard a knock on his door. "Come in," he called.

"I yoost came from da general store and dey are out of da rat poison. Dey vill order some more in da mornink," said Sven. "But da good news is da boys got a momma rat."

"I know, I saw it yesterday," commented the superintendent.

"I vouldn't vant to be around ven da mate, T-Rex, gets back t'ough," said Sven. "I hear he's a big von!" On that last comment Sven quickly slipped out the door. Nervously, Dr. Littleton started looking behind furniture, at baseboards and at his window.

It was 4 o'clock at the end of the day when Dr. Littleton's secretary knocked and poked her head in the door. "I'll be heading home now," she said, smiling. "Would you like me to lock up?"

"No. I have a few more notes to work on for Monday's meeting," replied Dr. Littleton, fussing with some papers. "You go on home. I'll close up tonight."

Dr. Littleton was so busy working on his speech that he hadn't noticed the darkness coming on or how late it was. All of a sudden he heard some scratching. His head snapped up and frantically looked left and right. Silence. It was eerie how quiet this building was when no one was around. He decided to lock the front door and headed to the front of the building. As soon as the door was locked he heard the scratching sound again. He cocked his head, listening for the sound as he walked back towards his office. He never made it to his office before the lights went completely dark. "What the....," he gulped. "Who turned off the lights!" Dr. Littleton went back to the door and flipped the light switch up and down. Nothing.

"We must have blown a fuse," he thought. "Now where did Sven say that flashlight was?" Dr. Littleton groped his way back to his office and found the closet. Inside was the flashlight, right where Sven put it.

"Sumptimes da old fuses blow an tif yoo are vorking late yoo'll vant dis flashlight here," Sven had said. Aah, the flashlight worked! Now where did Sven say that fuse box was?

"Der are some extra fuses in da fuse box in da basement," he remembered Sven saying. Using the flashlight he found the door to the basement. There was much squeaking as he opened the door. Afraid that someone might hear him, he stopped squeaking long enough to notice the door was squeaking, too.

"My, it certainly is da..dark down there," he said aloud. As he slowly crept down the stairs, the squeaking started again and this time the stairs joined him for a duet. When the excerpt was over he had reached the bottom of the stairs where he directed his flashlight around the room. It was filled with all kinds of artifacts. Old desks, chairs, boxes, a table saw, and many other items cluttered the basement.

He began walking away from the stairs and then caught a small panel door in the beam of the light in the far back of the room. He slowly crept back towards that panel when he began to hear the scratching again. It seemed to be coming from the direction of that panel. Sweat began to pour down Dr. Littleton's face. He then began to hear some squeaks and this time it wasn't him.

All of a sudden a hand touched his shoulder! He screamed and the flashlight flew out of his hand and crashed on the floor. "Who's there?" he yelled. Silence. After what seemed like an eternity, which in actuality was probably just a few seconds, Dr. Littleton reached out and touched the hand. However, it was no hand at all but some power cords hanging from a hook in the ceiling. "Whew," he thought as his heart slowed from its 190 pulses per minute. "Now where is that flashlight?"

Dr. Littleton groped around the floor, eventually locating the flashlight, which was utterly useless since the bulb broke when it was dropped. Fortunately, Dr. Littleton remembered the direction of the panel and headed that way, bumping his shins into chairs and desks, and cursing all the way. Finally, he touched the panel door and opened it. A small battery operated light turned on as he opened the door. "Oh, thank you, Sven!" he thought. He found the main light fuse, unscrewed it, and grabbed one of the fresh ones sitting just inside the panel." Just then he heard the squeak near his feet. As he looked down he caught the glow of the battery-operated light in two eyes, which were only two feet away. As he fumbled with the fuse the eyes began coming closer. Finally, he got the fuse screwed in. The lights came on in time for Dr. Littleton to be staring at the largest rat mankind had ever seen just one foot from where he was standing.

Dr. Littleton screamed. The muskrat squealed. That sent Dr. Littleton into a run that would have put any hurdler in awe. He was jumping over desks 4 feet at a hop, racing to the stairs. As he sprinted up the stairs he began screaming, "T-Rex! T-Rex!" When he got to the front door he fumbled at the lock and heard the squeaking right behind him, which of course, is always what the basement door does when the spring mechanism closes it. This caused him to scream even louder, "T-Rex! T-Rex! I just saw T-Rex!!"

As people were coming out of their houses to see what the commotion was they were introduced to the site of the superintendent running down main street screaming, "T-Rex! I just saw T-Rex!"

As far as we know, the superintendent never stopped running. At least, we never saw him in Lost Hollow again. Whenever conversation would steer towards the subject of the superintendent, heads would slowly shake and comments would be heard like, "….started seeing prehistoric dinosaurs…" or "..mad as a March hare…" or "…thought he was being chased by a Tyrannosaurus Rex…"

When Sven found the muskrat in the basement, the flashlight and pieces of Dr. Littleton's torn clothing, it was fairly obvious to him what happened. For that reason, the muskrat became a hero to all the school kids and teachers alike. So, at that Monday's school board meeting almost the entire town was there, casting their votes for our mascot to be the muskrat. From that time on we have been known as the Lost Hollow Muskrats, as terrifying as a T-Rex!

"You know," I said as I was munching on one of Mrs. Lindstrom's sugar-coated Rosettes, "I love Lumberjack Day!"

"You said it!" exclaimed Cranky, as we gazed across Lost Hollow from the top of the Ferris Wheel.

"Hey, you guys," said Tommy, pointing. "Let's try that new ride, next!"

"Sure," I said. "What's it called?"

Tommy replied, "It's called the T-Rex!"

THE BEGINNING BAND

"Keep your head down, Tom. How many can you make out?"

"Oh, about thirty-five. And they all got heavy-duty weapons. I think one even has a bassoon!"

"Do you mean bazooka, private?"

"No sir! I meant bassoon!"

So goes the nightmare before the first day of .... 'Beginning Band!' I thought I had gotten over those but they started recurring six days ago, which would be exactly one week before the first day of school.

For some band teachers there is nothing more dreaded than the first day of beginning band. Can you imagine 35 kids with what is tantamount to 35 weapons in their hands, aimed at you and not knowing how to use them? THAT can be a very dangerous situation. However, over the years I have learned to turn this situation into a positive event and have been able to quell most of my nerves, twitches and tics.

"Well, class, today you get to learn how to play an instrument!" I exclaimed encouragingly. Already a hand went up.

"Yes?" I asked.

"Mr. Olson," inquired a bright-eyed youngster, "my brother, Barney, says that we only get to learn how to open the case today like he did two years ago."

"Ah," I replied, "that was because half the band was drummers and oboe players and they needed some extra time learning how open their cases. "Besides," I thought, "since then I've learned how to quell most of my nerves, twitches, and tics."

At this point I must stress to the reader how important timing is to teaching. Knowing this I spent 15 minutes teaching how to open and close the case properly. That gave us about 25 minutes left in the class period.

"Now class, let's learn how to put the instruments together!"

"Yippee!" squealed 35 sixth graders. I was a little concerned about the drool coming out of the side of the mouths of two of the drummers.

"Here's how to do it class," I announced. "Open your books to page 2. Do you see the instructions and diagram? Well, read it and put those instruments together…..but DON'T PLAY!" The kids took the next two minutes and already had them together. They were supposed to take 5 minutes. Some of the kids were already starting to make noises with their instruments. So much for my timing.

"If anybody plays their instrument now they don't get to play it tomorrow!" I warned. Everybody was silent. "OK, kids, now take 'em apart." Groans and moans followed that statement.

"It's ok," I said, "we just need to practice this important part just a little." My timing was coming back.

"But Mr. Olson," retorted a trumpet player, "all we have to do with a trumpet is put the mouthpiece in it."

"Yes," I answered, "but I thought I saw someone putting his mouthpiece in backwards." Looking at their faces I realized that 6th graders could already perfect the skeptical look. "By the way, would you guys like to hear the story of the time the high school band learned how to march?"

"You're stalling, Mr. Olson!" came an exclamation from the back of the room. I was beginning to see a few mutinous looks from a number of the kids. I wondered if they had been hanging out with the 8th graders.

"It looks like everybody has the hang of it so it's time to actually make some sounds with our instruments."

"Yea!" squealed the class. More drool from the drum section…….

I looked at the clock and I could see we had just five minutes to go until the end of class.

"OK. Here is what we'll do. I am going to step into my office and close the door. The moment you hear the door close you start making sounds on your instrument, but NOT before you hear the door close! Then when you see the principal run in, stop playing. Everybody got it?"

"Yes, Mr. Olson." What a great class.

"Now repeat the instructions to your neighbors until you're sure they understand."

The clock said one minute left to go. As I walked toward my office one of the kids asked, "What are you putting in your ears, Mr. Olson?"

Ignoring this I said, "Now wait until you hear my office door close."

Just then the principal walked in to the band room. "Mr. Togglemeyer," I yelled, "don't let that door clos……"

At that moment the most horrific torrent of screeching, squealing, and yelping was heard. Most of it seemed to be coming from Mr. Togglemeyer but the band was holding its own and was almost deafening, even with my earplugs in. I just reached my office and slammed the door with poor Mr. Togglemeyer writhing and trying to get in. Somehow, I must have accidentally locked my door. But before I could open it, Mr. Togglemeyer, was already passed out on the floor. Of course, nobody saw the principal come in, which would have been their cue to stop playing. The class kept playing and playing their instruments, not hearing the bell, for about an hour. Nobody was willing to open the door of the band room and I certainly was not going out there into that! Well, actually, I DID go out and drag poor Mr. Togglemeyer into the hallway and quite possibly saved his life. I was surprised I never received a medal for that.

Eventually, the kids' lip muscles gave out and they stopped playing except for the entire drum section, which might have renovated the definition for Neanderthal. By grabbing each kid's sticks away I finally got them quieted down, also.

"Where are they, sergeant?"

"I think they are in that trench, sir."

"About how many?"

"Could be a hundred, sir."

Three to one odds, I thought. Not impossible but it would have been better if WE were the three.

"Alright, people. Let 'em have it!" I barked.

The clarinets started sending them a screaming volley. The trumpets followed with a blast of their weapons. Then, the heavy artillery of tubas, bass clarinets and baritone saxophones launched a barrage. The enemy cowered. When the percussion unleashed its barrage, that did it!

"They're retreating, sir!"

"After them!" I shouted, and leapt out of the trench on a dead run. I took two steps and fell flat on my face in the mud.

"Get up, sir!" shouted the sergeant. "Get up!"

I tried to struggle to my feet but my legs wouldn't move.

"Get up, Greg! Get up!"

I opened my eyes to see Cranky staring down at me, coffee breath and all.

"Huh?" I said, intelligently.

"Hurry, Greg, or you'll be late to the second day of school!" he exclaimed, hurriedly.

"Sorry," I replied. "I didn't sleep much last night."

I got ready as fast as I could and as we raced out the front door I began thinking of the previous day. I was reminded about the sound created by the Beginning Band yesterday and some positives that resulted from that. For one, the principal rarely bothers me in my room anymore. Secondly, I recorded that sound and put it on my answering machine. I get so few solicitor calls these days.

IN THE CORPS STYLE

In this dog-eat-dog world there are people who get up early, stay late, meet in committees, grab quick meals, and take work home to finish before doing it all again the next day. These people are called marching band students.

High schools all across the United States have had marching bands in their tradition almost as long as football teams. Until the 1970s many marching bands used what is called the "high-step" style of marching. Now more bands use what is called "corps style" marching, which intends to keep the upper torso as motionless as possible so that playing of instruments is better controlled. Of course, the assumption is that band students can control their instruments before they begin to march. How did anybody come to that conclusion?

This is a story of an event that took place early in my career as a band teacher. This is NOT the story of how I was coerced into taking over the band position, even though my major in college was history. I should never have played that little guitar piece for my principal......but I digress. Here is the story about how the marching band got started at Lost Hollow High School.

One day I was approached by Mayor Jon Eriksson and my principal, who asked if I would field a marching band during the half time of the homecoming football game.

"Olson," the mayor orated, "some of the leaders in our town have been complaining about the fact that we don't have a band marching in the half times. Those same leaders are the ones who donate funds during the sports banquets and help us pass those levies. Do you think you're getting my drift?"

I stood there with a blank stare. Or it was at least as blank as I could make it. I had practiced it at the mirror until I thought it was perfected.

"Don't give us that blank stare, Olson," the principal warned, "I've seen you use that before and I know you understand what we are saying!"

Maybe I should have used the I-feel-ill-right-now technique. Naturally, I wanted to support our school in spite of the countless extra hours of rehearsal and drill, the expense, the whining from the flutes, and the fact that real humans would actually be watching and listening. So I offered the following speculations: "You know, the kids might catch cold in the night air, the cold might damage the trombones, and the noise from the drummers might upset the neighboring communities."

In his usually sympathetic way I was encouraged by my principal: "Either have a band performing in the next football home game's half time or you get to run the detention room!" Maybe chocolate would postpone the whining from the flutes.

One thing was for sure. To avoid an all-out mutiny from the band members I would have to use all of my tactfulness-skills on springing this news to my wary students. I decided that my first act would be to look up the word, tactfulness.

"Band," I bemoaned on the next day near the end of the rehearsal, "we have a wonderful opportunity coming our way." There was a look of dread from the clarinet section.

"You're not going to teach the "water key" lesson again, are you?" probed a doubtful clarinet player.

"…or plan to have us mow lawns in the winter like last year?" questioned one of the anti-fundraising trombonists.

"…or perform for the school board's annual potluck again? Only two school board members showed up!"

"Now, now, munchkins, I am simply talking about something that will not only be a musical venture but entertaining as well." I could tell that I was beginning to gain their confidence by the way they were eyeing me suspiciously. Usually they would eye me suspiciously AND frown. They hadn't started frowning yet.

"I can tell by the way you are eyeing me suspiciously that you would like to know more," I explained. "I have decided that your musical education has been lacking an element of musicality called movement."

"Movement?" eyed a skeptical drummer, "How is that a musical element?"

"You know I've always said the you should move to the music. And now you are going to get the opportunity."

"Are you talking about doing marching?" inquired a soon-to-be-whining flute player.

Whoa. That question came way too soon! I just knew I should have sent the flutes to the library to do research. I could tell that I now had to come up with something fast by the way the percussion section was eyeing me suspiciously AND frowning.

"Actually, I am honoring a request that you made a while ago. You said that you would like to go outside and play." I replied apprehensively.

"That was last spring," nullified a saxophonist, "and the weather was warmer then. This is the fall and it's cold outside!"

"Hey, I didn't say you couldn't wear a coat." I soothed.

Here I should pause and point out that the essence of all good teaching is instructional timing. The next thing that happened proved that point. The bell rang.

"Looks like we will have to continue this discussion tomorrow." I mentioned cheerily. "Don't forget to bring your coat!"

The next day I stopped off at the local bakery before heading to school. I purchased what I call "educational reinforcement." At school the band kids showed up, most of them wearing light coats. The flute section, however, had on sweaters, ski parkas, balaclavas, and ski hats.

"Don't you think you've overdone it a little?" I wondered as I eyed their ski poles nervously. "What are those poles for?"

"We brought these in case you have us do a lot of hiking."

I wasn't sure whether she meant she would use them during hiking or use them on whoever proposed doing the hiking.

"Mr. Olson, why does it smell like a bakery in here?" inquired an olfactorous tuba player.

"Well, class. Lets head out and meet on the football field," I chimed. There was absolutely no movement...except their eyebrows...ALL of their eyebrows, which were moving into the shape of a frown. I couldn't see the flute players' eyebrows, however, behind those balaclavas.

I exclaimed, "The first ten students to the 50 yard line get doughnuts!"

It pays to have foresight. It also helps that band is just before lunch. The only thing that slowed the kids down was the bottleneck at the door. Of course, band kids are more polite than others. There was only pulling, shoving, clawing, gouging, karate, but NO tripping. Non-band kids would have included the tripping. I had to smile, as I was quite impressed with the technique exhibited by the flute players with those ski poles.

Out on the fifty-yard line, on which the band kids were standing, one could see the frost that covered the entire football field. I winced, thinking about what it was going to be like when the snow came.

"Why are you wincing, Mr. Olson?" asked one of the closer students.

"It's OK," I said, "it's just an old war injury and is usually only painful when I exercise or if students ask too many questions."

"Where are the doughnuts, Mr. Olson?" asked the same impertinent student, trying to get me to wince.

"You get them at the END of the class period. You remember what happens to the inside of your instrument when you eat food just before you play? Or do you want me to teach THAT lesson again?"

"No! Mr. Olson, no!" came the unanimous response along with a look of trepidation (except from the ninja-clad flutes).

"Speaking of instruments, Mr. Olson, in our hurry to get out here we forgot to bring them."

"That's fine. You won't need them today." I responded.

Grumble, grumble, grumble.

"Today, you get to learn corp-style mar…, er, walking!" One has to choose words carefully with a class like this. "People, I want you to move your left foot forward like this." I took one step towards them with my left foot. In response, about two-thirds of them took a step towards me with their right. I stood there with my mouth open. "Go back to the fifty-yard line and let's try it again. Grumble, grumble, grumble.

This time I faced away from them, took a step with my left and turned my head to see the result. This time all the students except Tommy Feldman (who was also known as Blap) took a step with their left. "Would somebody show Blap which foot is his left? We have to do it over again!" Grumble, grumble, grumble.

"Mr. Olson, I think we would be more willing if you didn't grumble so much!" came a retort from one of the students.

Over the course of the next 4 school days it became apparent that there was no way we would be ready to do a half time show by the next home game, which was only another week away. This called for drastic measures. Drastic measures quite often meant enlisting the aid of Mr. Cranklemeyer, the PE teacher. Approximately fifty percent of the time, aid coming from Mr. Cranklemeyer has ended up in the disaster category. However, the other half of his schemes border on the category of genius. Right now I could see there being a 100 percent chance of disaster without some help. I could only hope that this was one of Mr. Cranklemeyer's lucky halves.

"Hey, Cranky!" I chortled during lunch. "I'll bet you haven't been challenged to a game of chance in a long time." Mr. Cranklemeyer was an incessant gambler.

"Oh, no you don't, Olson! The last time you made that statement my car ended up in Florida!"

"Now, now, Cranky. This day and age Florida is not really that far from Washington State. Besides, I have a wager that is a piece of pie!"

"Cake."

"What?"

"Cake! Piece of cake!"

"No thanks. I already had dessert." You know, a frown from a teacher looks quite a bit like a frown from a student.

"Anyway, the wager is simple. All it amounts to is this: if you lose, you figure out a way to make my band look and sound great for the first ever half time show we have ever done."

At first I thought that I had lost the genius-half of Cranky because he just sat there staring two double-aught holes through me for about 15 seconds. Then, all-of-a-sudden a roar of laughter exploded from his mouth, which lasted much more than 15 seconds.

"OK, Cranky. As soon as you are done…"

Roar…roar…

"All right, then…"

"Har-de-har…"

"Cranky!" I yelled. "The kids don't really have to play their instruments. I figure we can put a recording on the loudspeaker and have the kids fake it. My problem is that they can't march and I only have a week left to go."

"Snicker, snicker."

"Besides, I am willing to wager my collector's edition 1962 Gibson Les Paul."

Instantly, there was focus in Cranky's demeanor. I knew his weak spot was for guitars and especially for my 1962 Gibson, which he talked about at many of our lunch periods.

"Let me get this straight," said Cranky. "You're betting your Gibson but if I lose I help your kids get through this half time show looking like stars?"

"That's the long and short of it." I beamed.

"And what kind of game are playing for this wager?" probed Cranky.

I said, "It's a number game. I write a number on a piece of paper and you guess a number between 1 and 10. Then we have a bystander choose a number. If you are the closest then you win. If the bystander is closest I win."

Cranky squinted at me as he said, "That SOUNDS fair enough but where's the catch?"

"Catch?" I said, painfully. "The catch is a 1962 Gibson Les Paul."

Ah, the weak spot.

"OK, Olson, write down the number," Cranky said as he watched me through narrow slits.

I found a piece of paper and holding it below the table I wrote down the number, folded it in half and put my coffee cup on it. "What number do you choose, Cranky?"

"Five!" he said with a smirk. "Now I'll have a fifty-fifty chance."

"Who should call the number for me, Cranky?"

Just then Miss Snaggel, the math teacher sat down. "Miss Snaggel," said Cranky, "would you mind helping us with a little math problem?"

I quickly announced, "We need you to choose a number between 1 and 100," I said to Miss Snaggel as Cranky stared at me with his mouth open.

"OK." She said, thinking a few seconds.

"But, but, but…." sputtered Cranky.

"I'll choose 74," said Miss Snaggel.

"Wait a minute," I blurted out. "I got it wrong. You have to choose a number between one and ten."

"Ha, ha!" exclaimed Cranky, always looking for a chance to get ahead. "You can't change your instructions now! You gave them to her and now you have to live with them! Where is that Gibson?"

"But can this be fair?" I asked.

"It IS fair because YOU were the one who asked her to choose a number between 1 to 100!" exclaimed Cranky, with a gleam in his eye.

"If you say so, Cranky," I acceded. "Miss Snaggel, would you mind checking that number under the coffee cup?

Miss Snaggel lifted the coffee cup and opened up the sheet of paper. "Why, it has the number 99 on it!"

"What?" yelled Cranky, with gleamless eyes. "You were supposed to write a number between 1 and 10."

"Actually, I never said I was going to WRITE a number between 1 and 10. I just wanted you to choose one," I stated as sauntered towards the door. Had I mentioned that Cranky played nose guard for the WSU football team? As timing would have it the bell rang to signal the end of lunch. And did I also mention the importance of timing? As I slid through the door I would have sworn I heard roar of some prehistoric animal. I figured tomorrow would be a better day to collect on our little wager.

In the morning before school there was a T-Rex drinking coffee in our staff lounge. "Cranky," I called cheerily, "I hope you had a chance to think about our band's half time show."

"Actually, I did," growled the dinosaur. "and I came up with a plan where your kids don't even have to march."

"But the principal said….," I began.

"…said they had to 'perform'," he went on. "According to what you told me he did not say they had to march."

"What are you thinking, Cranky?"

"Do you know that 4-wheel ATV club I belong to? I think we can get the club to hook up some of the flat beds down at Floyd's Rental Shop to their rigs. Floyd's one of the members so I called him. He has already agreed to let us use 'em. We can have the kids sitting on the flat beds while we haul them around the field. What do you think about that?" charged Cranky.

In my usual supportive way I said, "That has got to be one of the most preposterous, ridiculous, obtuse, reckless, and slipshod things you have ever come up with, Cranky! Do you think we ought to practice it once?"

"No, no!" rebutted Cranky. "The kids only have to sit on the flatbeds pretending to play their instruments. There is no need to practice."

"What about the drivers?" I probed.

Cranky responded, "I'll draw up a map of patterns that will show where they go and it will look great. We've done this kind of thing for years at various parades!"

Knowing this to be true and remembering how impressed I was seeing the club in action at the local parade I said with an ear-to-ear grin, "Cranky, I think you are a genius!"

"So you don't think I could just hold that Gibson of yours?" inquired Cranky. "And by the way, how do you get your grin to go from ear-to-ear like that?"

There was a positive and a negative for the night of the football game. The positive was that it was not snowing or even very cold. The negative was that it was pouring down rain like cats and dogs. Actually, there were no cats and dogs. They were smart enough to stay in covered areas. The mayor and principal must have learned something from those animals because they were in the enclosed press box. "Well Olson," charged the mayor, "shouldn't you be down there with your band?"

"Actually, I need to be high up here to see the patterns created by the formations," I said dryly.

"I just hope your kids are going to give us a night to remember!" exclaimed Mayor Eriksson.

"I am sure they will be wonderful!" exclaimed the principal who was looking at me much the way a fox looks at a rabbit.

"Me too," I shuddered, much in the way a rabbit looks at a fox.

I could see that the game clock was down to one minute left in the half. I could also see the 4-wheelers with flat beds attached sitting at both ends of the field ready to enter. Upon the flatbeds were placed chairs on which sat the band kids in uniform. At least I thought they were my band kids. They looked more like drenched cats and dogs. Just then my walkie-talkie radio went off. "Eagle 1 this is Fox 1!"

"Cranky," I said, "can we dispense with the call signs. We are not at war here…at least not yet."

"The ATVs are ready. Are you set with the music up there?" asked Cranky wetly.

"It's ready to go, Cranky. Good luck!" I said dryly. Just then the gun went off to mark the end of the 1st half of the game. "Here we go!" I heard crackling over the radio. With a signal from Cranky, the ATVs started rolling. And I started the recording of Tchaikovsky's 1812 Overture.

I might mention that the rain had created some fairly large puddles all over the field. The first puddle that was hit by a 4-wheeler created a big splash that sprayed ten feet high in which was caught the light from the big field spots. The effect was to create a rainbow of dazzling colors. The ooh's and ahh's of the crowd were quite audible as splash after splash of amazing color blossomed over the field. I don't think I have ever seen anything so beautiful on a football field. And the amazing thing is that the splashes coincided with the big booms and crashes from the 1812 Overture.

"That's gorgeous!" exclaimed my principal.

"Ingenious!" shouted the mayor.

I was beginning to think my job was still safe when it happened. The first 4-wheeler that came onto the field had swerved to miss one of the big puddles and almost lost the kids off his flatbed.

"How do you have those chairs attached to the flatbeds?" shouted my principal through the powerful sounds of the 1812 coming over the loudspeaker.

"With duct tape!" I yelled back.

"In this rain?" bellowed the principal.

Too late I saw his reasoning. A second 4-wheeler swerved to avoid a collision with the first swerving ATV. The effect was to release four duct-taped chairs with students from the flatbed into the puddle he was trying to miss. The spray must have propelled fifteen feet into the air. "Ooh!" shouted the audience. Unfortunately, the spray covered a third driver's goggles with mud, who ran into another 4-wheeler. Both sets of chairs lost the hold of duct tape, which propelled both sets of band kids into more puddles creating a double explosion of color. "Aah! exclaimed the crowd.

I was just beginning to think this was not too bad when one of the ATVs careened off the grass, trying to avoid another vehicle, and running along the track in front of the stands. Here I might mention that having your umbrella OVER your head might not be the best location for it. That was proven by most of the town council, teachers, band parents and their families as the spray from the track drenched the bottom four rows of the bleachers. Not hearing any more oohs and ahhs I felt that I had stayed dry enough and should be outside with my band and quickly slipped out of the press box. As I headed for the back gate I would have sworn I heard "Olson" being yelled through the loud speaker.

Once again, timing had proven to be with me. I had reached the back gate without anyone spotting me. But more importantly, one of the fortunate things about high school football games is that many of them are played on Fridays. With two personal leave days taken that meant I wouldn't have to show up to school for another five days, which I considered a nice cooling off period. Adding three sick days would be just about right. These were the thoughts I had the next morning as my wife Darla and I were driving up to Canada for a little vacation.

From the passenger side Darla exclaimed, "Isn't that beautiful!" She was looking past me out my side window. Wouldn't you know it, as I looked to my left I could see over the Puget Sound one of the most beautiful rainbows I'd ever witnessed! I began whistling the "1812 Overture."

HOW TO FAKE IT

No matter how large the music ensemble, there comes a time where your individual musicianship (or lack thereof) will be on display. In a concert there might be many people in the audience watching you but if you are savvy they will never know it's YOU that made that mistake. Younger students usually take a while to master the art of faking it. Quite often, in a beginning band performance you might see an instrumentalist display his/her frustration at missing a note or, even worse, start laughing. They just haven't realized that the audience has heard so many wrong notes from the beginning band that they would never have known who it was except for the animated behavior of that individual. Eventually, as they become more musically mature they learn better ways of faking it.

Of course, in the rehearsal is where someone's true "fake it" technique gets a workout. In the typical rehearsal a director might stop and have a section of the band, for example the clarinets, play a particular passage of the music. Here is where expertise really comes into play. Expertise on how to fake it, I mean. There are different styles of faking it and I would like to take a moment to discuss some of them. Here is a listing of the different styles:

Strong Silent Type. I remember having the trumpet section play a segment of Beethoven's 9th Symphony. As they played the part you would have thought, by looking at them, they all had it mastered. They were all sitting with good posture, mouthpieces to their lips, fingers moving and breathing together. The music sounded flawless. However, even though there were nine of them it sounded more like two or three. When finished, all nine sat back with confident smiles. Now, I KNOW that there were only two or three actually playing but I had to hand it to those trumpeters. They showed some of the best "fake-it" technique I had ever seen.

Next we have the **Accusers**. However, there are sub-categories to this style so I will list each one separately.

Accuser: Eye-Roll. One day, I was having the band play part of a song when there was a huge squeak out of the saxophone section. As I stopped the band and looked at the saxophones, all of them, even the section-leader, was looking at me then rolling their eyes to the person sitting next to them. Some of them could even roll their eyes while applying the slight-nod-of-head-to-the-side-the-culprit-is-on technique. The effect was to have a bunch of jerking heads in the middle of the band, which made it almost impossible not to burst out laughing. The rest of the band kids were a little more serious. They would eye these saxophonists and critique their style. "I give that one 9.5," a trombonist might say to his partner. "Naw, she jerks her head to much….needs to be more subtle. "She gets a '7'," would say the partner.

Accuser: Turn head. This technique seems to be used by a lot of flutists and percussion players. Maybe that's because the nature of their instruments allows for more movement. A flutist, who misses a fingering, will sometimes be seen immediately turning her head and then staring at the oblivious girl next to her. The ones who have really practiced this technique will even catch the director's eye and shake their heads as if to say, "You and I sure put up with a lot, don't we?"

Accuser: Aggressive. This person uses the swat-the-neighbor's-arm-with-back-of-hand approach. Typically, the person who uses this approach is MUCH larger than the recipient of the technique.

Bathroom Pass Style. Sometimes there is no getting around it. Eventually, the director will have every individual in the section play the passage. At the point that this becomes a strong possibility the savvy student uses the bathroom pass just before his/her turn to play.

I Feel Sick. This is sometimes thought of as a subdivision of the Bathroom Pass Style. However, because one can be gone for an indefinite amount of time to the nurse it is considered MUCH more powerful and should be used sparingly.

My Reed Just Broke Technique. If the director is having everyone in the section play a passage individually and someone has already gotten to the bathroom pass first, then this technique is usually foolproof. When the director says, "Jimmy, show us how to play the passage," then the response, "my reed just broke and I don't have another," works quite well. Of course, this is the point where brass players become disgusted with woodwinds. Some very jealous brass players will even try to emulate the woodwinds by saying something like, "I forgot my mouthpiece," but that is just too obvious and would get a poor score in "fake it" technique. Percussion players eventually learn NOT to say, "I forgot my sticks," because a savvy director will say, "Well then, just use your hands!"

My Instrument Just Broke. Again, this is a variation of the My Reed Just Broke Technique. Experienced fakers know how to move a spring, switch valves or similar procedures in order to make it look authentic.

I would like to say that this is a complete list of Fake-It techniques, however, students can be very creative and I am sure this list will grow over time. You might even know of a technique that is not listed. If you do, please do not share with me and especially do NOT share it with my students. I can't quite keep up with the ones they already know!

The only thing I think I need to add here is that some have spent much time developing these skills. In fact, so much time has been spent in their mastery that one might wonder how come they didn't spend that much time … practicing.

DOWNBEATER

In music performance, whether it be professional or amateur, there are musicians of various personality types. Stereotypes emerge in the music community and perhaps you have read some jokes based on those stereotypes. There is one personality type, however, for which I would like to expound: The Downbeater.

The Downbeater has acquired his/her name by showing up just slightly before the downbeat for the first note of a performance. Usually, the Downbeater leaves home at the last possible moment to get to the concert 5 minutes before the downbeat. Of course, this same person hopes that there won't be some unplanned flat tire, traffic snarl, or bakery on the way to the performance. Sometimes the Downbeater plans to leave early for the show but keeps finding more little jobs to do and eventually leaves late anyway.

I would like the reader to know that I am NOT one of those kinds of people. The few times that I showed up just before the downbeat were situations that were out of my control. For example, there was the time that the black bear got trapped in my basement just before the Winter Concert. And once, when Lost Hollow's power went out, Tom Brandston accidentally lit the principal's pickup on fire. But that's a very long story. And then there was the time that was completely John Cranklemeyer's fault. I thought I would tell you about it here.

"Cranky," as his friends know him, has taught P.E. at Lost Hollow High School and has been a good friend....mostly. He persuaded me to join him on a little fishing trip on the same day as our Spring Concert. I remember our conversation in the faculty room the day before the concert.

"Come on, Greg. It's just a little creek that runs into the Stagomish River and it's only ten miles from Lost Hollow."

"I don't know, Cranky," I said, "I've never gone fishing on the same day as a concert."

"Look, school gets out at three, he continued, "and we could be on the road in fifteen minutes. We'll be there by four o'clock, in time for the best fishing we have had in 5 years."

"Yeah?" I asked with squinting eyes. Cranky had sparked my curiosity.

"Yeah," he continued, "and the salmon are as plentiful as I have ever seen. We'll have our limit by five and be back in Lost Hollow no later than 5:30 PM. By the way, why are you squinting? Is the light too bright in here?"

Cranky sat back as if he had just finished making an advertising proposal to some company CEO. As I watched him chomp down on his sandwich I began thinking of the reports of the Chinook run on the Stagomish. A 21 pounder was caught just yesterday.

"If we were to get back by 5:30 that would be plenty of time before the 7:30 performance and would even give me a couple of hours leeway time," I thought out loud.

"Absolutely!" said Cranky, standing up. "Well, I've got to get to my next class. I'll pick you up at 3:15 tomorrow."

"But, but…" It was too late. He was out the door of the faculty room.

In the school parking lot the next day, as I was getting my tackle out of my car, the principal pulled along side me in his pickup. "Watcha got all that fishing gear for, Greg?" he inquired. "You goin' to be fishing for some right notes at your concert this year? Har, har de har…." He sped off to his parking spot without waiting for a reply. When I got to my room I put the fishing gear in my office. My day, which included dress rehearsals and concert set-up, went as smooth as a salmon gliding through a slow moving creek. That should have been a sign to me. I typically only get so much smooth in a day.

I was just locking up the door to the band room when I heard honking from Cranky's 4x4. When I came out Cranky said, "If it wasn't for this little problem I'd be ready to shove off."

"What's the problem?" I asked, squinting again.

"Well," he answered, with apprehension written on his face, "my fan belt is a bit loose and frayed. It looks as though it might break at any moment. But it'll probably get us to the creek and back. By the way, you're squinting again. Do you think you need to get your eyes checked?"

I knew he was trying to get me to use my car. But the apprehension written on his face had me a little unnerved. If he would have had concern or unease written there, or even nervousness, I would have been resolute for taking his pickup. But 'apprehension' always gets me.

"Well, I suppose we could take my car," I responded, still squinting. "How bad is the road to the creek?" I knew that the road to the river was not great but I was able to drive there in my car before. But I had never been to this creek.

"It's a piece of cake," said Cranky, "much like the river road."

I had never considered the river road a "piece of cake" so that description gave me a little trepidation.

"I don't know," I said, trying to hide my trepidation.

"You've got trepidation written all over your face," he said. "You don't have to worry. Remember? I've already been there! By the way, if you don't stop squinting your face is going to set like that permanently." The smile he gave me should have tipped me off. The right side of his mouth twitched which is generally a dead give-away. That usually happened only when there was something he wasn't telling me.

"On the road Cranky asked, "What size tires do you have on this car, anyway?"

"I've got 15's," I replied. "Why?"

"Just wondering."

The look on his face was a little disconcerting. I don't know what gave me more concern on that trip, the actual events or his questions on the way. At any rate, we eventually reached the river road and turned off the highway. I managed to maneuver around the potholes, ponds, gates and even the washed away sections of the river road.

"You might need to slow down a little here, said Cranky. "We're almost to the end of the good section of road."

"GOOD section!?" I exclaimed.

"Slow down a little," said Cranky. "The turn off for the creek is up here a little ways and if you're going too fast you'll miss it."

"I'm only going 5 miles an hour."

"I know. Slow down." Eventually he exclaimed, "There it is!"

"Where? I don't see a road."

"Right there! See those two tracks? I made those myself the last time I was here."

I could barely make out the tire marks. They seemed to go down a little hill on both sides of a bush that looked to be three feet tall. "You took your truck down there?" I said, incredulously.

"Yep. It's better than it looks. That bush will just bend over as you go over it."

"Cranky, that's no road. That's a trail!"

"It USED to be a trail but I made it into a road. Now let's get going before it gets too late!" Cranky barked. His frown seemed to say, "You're not going to wimp out on me?"

"I'm NOT a wimp!" I barked.

"Wha…," he began. But he didn't have time to finish his sentence because I gunned the motor and off we went. About six feet, that is. We became high-centered on that bush. It began to rain.

"Oh, great!" I exclaimed, with anger-frustration-dismay.

Not wanting to be around anger-frustration-dismay for very long Cranky said, "Why don't you get out and see what's holding us."

"I KNOW what's holding us! It's that monster bush you said would bend!"

"Maybe it's just snagged on the bumper?"

"Oh alright!" I said in frustration as I climbed out of the car. Once I got outside I realized Cranky could have come out in the rain just as well as me. I looked under the car and there was the bush, dead center of a high-centered car. It looked as though it had hardly bent at all. As I walked up to the door, there was Cranky, sitting in the driver's side.

"What are you doing!?" I yelled at the rolled up window.

A muffled response came from the window, "If I try rocking the car with the accelerator and you try lifting up on the back end we can probably get over this bush."

"Why don't YOU come out and lift it!" I hollered.

"There's no need for both of us to get wet!" came the reply, accentuated with a frown.

As I traipsed back to the rear of the car I was so mad that the raindrops instantly turned into steam as they hit my head. "Ready, go!" I yelled as I began lifting up on the bumper.

"Cranky moved the car forward slightly then quickly released the clutch, and the car rolled back. He continued this back and forth motion, rocking the car as I lifted. As I was beginning to give up hope the car began to ease a little farther forward and then shot ahead, leaving me face down in the mud. I stood up slowly looking like MudMan, a new superhero. MudMan was about to rid Lost Hollow of one of its evil P.E. teachers. As I trudged up to the car, Cranky had already slid into the passenger side. I climbed in.

"What's been taking you so long?" he quipped. "We gotta get to the fishing spot before this rain starts churning up the mud." He then noticed my state of dress. "Whoa!" he said. "You've gotta be a little more careful. It's slippery out there, ya know?"

Cranky must have noticed my hands looking a little like vice-grips because he quickly said. "Now step on it!"

As the car moved forward I was straining to see out of my windshield as I dodged trees, potholes, bushes, and now ditches, created by the rain.

"This is it!" shouted Cranky, grabbing his gear. He shot out of the door and got into position with his fly pole. I set the parking brake, grabbed my gear and walked down beside him. As I looked around I noticed this section of the creek was lined by overhanging vine maple trees. The only area that was opened to casting was the spot Cranky was standing in right now.

"And where am I to fish?" I asked in frustration.

"How about that spot over there?" he replied, motioning with his thumb. The area he indicated was a 3-foot by 3-foot clearing underneath five different types of trees. He continued, "If you use the side-arm technique it will work perfectly." I was thinking of a side-arm technique I could use on Cranky when two things happened simultaneously.

One was something hit Cranky's line so hard he almost lost his pole. His pole was bobbing up and down wildly with such complex rhythms he could have been first-chair drummer in my band. As he yelled, "Whooee! Got one on!" I had noticed some movement out of the corner of my eye.

The movement that I perceived was the other thing happening. My car started rolling, no, sliding down the hill. The wheels weren't moving at all. It seemed the entire area where my car was standing was sliding down the hill, mud and all, heading right for the stream.

"EEEK!" I screamed.

"I know," said Cranky, smiling in his excitement. "Isn't it a beaut!"

"It's moving! It's moving!" I shrieked, as I ran for my car.

"I see it!" Cranky shouted. "I'm giving him a little more slack."

"My car, bumblebrain!" I shouted, desperately, as I started trying to pull back on the rear bumper.

Cranky turned around and saw my car for the first time, about twenty feet from the creek. That was about the same distance the salmon was from the shore. He looked at the salmon, then back at the car, then back to the salmon.

"Pull!" he shouted as he tightened the drag and brought the fish closer.

"Cranky!" I bellowed. "Get over here, now!"

Cranky frantically moved his head towards the car, then the fish, then back and forth two more times.

"Cranky!" I yelled.

"Oh, drat!" he hollered as he threw down his pole and came running. On the way he grabbed a good sized branch resting on the ground. In one huge motion he swung the branch down to a space just before the front right tire. Clunk! The car stopped its downward slide.

"Whew!" I breathed.

"Whew!" Cranky breathed.

"One more minute and we would have had to float back to town," I said, smiling.

"We may have to do just that!" Cranky rebutted. "There is no way you're going to get this car back up that hill."

As I took in the entire picture of our predicament I stated, "If you would have driven your 4x4 we would not be stuck like this!"

"If you have forgotten, you volunteered to take your car."

"What'll we do, now?" I asked, as I looked at my watch. "Oh, great! It's already 5:00! How am I going to get to the concert on time without a car?"

"If we walk out to the highway, we can hitchhike," said Cranky.

"Well, let's get going, now!" I commanded.

As I turned to go up the hill I heard, "Look!"

There was Cranky chasing his fishing pole, which was hopping and bouncing over the rocks alongside the creek. Cranky reached the pole and shouted, "He's still on!" as he began reeling in.

Eventually, he said, "Grab the net!" I retrieved the net and as the fish drew closer Cranky said, "Not yet…. Not yet…. Now!" I dropped the net below the surface of the water and at that same moment the fish darted to my left. I swung to my left so that the fish would swim into the net thereby losing my balance and falling headlong into the creek. Cranky's hand pulled me out as he said, "Will you stop horsing around!" But when he noticed I still had the net-with-fish in my hands he clapped me on the shoulder and said, "Great tackle!" On the shore Cranky was holding a Chinook that had to weigh at least 20 pounds.

"What a great day!" exclaimed Cranky. I was personally having a hard time with that statement.

We decided to lock our gear in the trunk of the car before heading toward the highway. He wouldn't leave the salmon, though. After he cleaned it, he put it in the fish bag that was attached to his fishing vest and we headed up the hill.

"At least you're not muddy anymore!" he said, unaware of the danger he was in earlier with MudMan. We made it to the River Road.

"Cranky, it's another mile-and-a-half to the highway and it's getting close to 6 o'clock," I lamented.

Cranky responded, "See that gate up there? We can save a half hour or more by cutting across this farmer's land."

"You mean the gate that's standing next to the 'DANGER – NO TRESPASSING' sign?"

"Sure! This farmer probably just wants to keep this secret fishing hole to himself so he's just trying to scare off his competition."

As we walked across the farmland, a mist started to move in with the breeze.

"This fog chills me to the bone," I said, shivering.

"That's because you're all wet," came the reply. "Here take this." Cranky took off his coat and I was beginning to see him in a new light, until he also took off his fishing vest and handed it to me instead of the coat. As I took it from him he said, "Careful not to drop the fish." The vest did add a little warmth but it also added 20 lbs. to the left side of my body. "You're squinting again," Cranky observed.

As we crested a little hill the mist began to dissipate. We looked down and saw approximately 30 bison, which many people tend to call buffalo.

"Uh, Cranky. Let's silently go back the way we came," I whispered, anxiously.

"You'll never make it to the concert," he whispered back. "We could slip through that way." He was pointing at a 20-foot wide clearing between two groups of the animals.

Nervously, I whispered, "You lead the way." We carefully walked as silently and slowly as we could, trying not to arouse the herd's attention. However, I think Cranky didn't understand about the silent part because he managed to bring down his boots on every twig or branch within stepping distance.

"Hmmph."

"What did you say?" whispered Cranky.

"I didn't say anything."

"Hmmph." "Hmmph."

Of course, it was the bison. They were probably saying, " You have encroached upon our territory without permission, have ignored the no trespassing sign, and now we are going to trample you into fine dust." I was a bit rusty with my buffalo translation and so mistook it to mean, "We see that you are just passing through, so please be our guest and may we get you anything?"

"Hmmph." "Hmmph, Hmmph." "Hmmph."

"…er, Cranky." As I turned to look at Cranky, he was at full speed, heading towards the nearest fence. I turned back to see about 15 bison heads, whose eyes seemed to turn magically red, with fire coming out of their nostrils, and smiling. Seeing the smiling part, I took off at a dead run. With the 20 lbs. of salmon weighing me down it was more like a deadly run.

Cranky, who I could see was sitting on top of the log fence, was shouting encouragement, "Run! But don't drop the fish!"

If it wasn't for that fish I think I would have made the fence. However, at just about five feet short a horn caught my right rear pocket and helped me clear the fence by an easy 4 feet. As Cranky helped me to my feet he said, "Wow! Touchdown and no fumble!" He had noticed the salmon still in the fish bag. "I wish you were on my team!" We turned to see my assailant on the other side of the fence with a patch of blue cloth on one of his horns.

Fortunately, we did not have to wait on the highway very long for a ride to town. Jerry McNaughten, the pig farmer, was on his way back to his farm after making a purchase of a hog at the county fair.

"Whooee," he said. "You can't ride in here with that fish. Climb in back."

I hopped up onto the truck bed and met Wilford, Jerry's new hog, who cuddled up and basically pinned me to a corner. Cranky sat up front with Jerry. By the time we reached town it was 7:20 PM. The concert was to start in 10 minutes.

"I won't have even enough time for a shower!" I cried.

"You'll be ok," said Cranky. "Here give me the fish and then GO!" He took the vest from me.

As I ran into the band room I saw all the kids, in their uniforms, staring at me with their mouths hanging open. I didn't realize it at the time but what they saw in the doorway was a semi-human form, streaked with mud and smelling of fish and pig.

"Eeyoo! What's that smell?" asked the conscientious flute players.

"No time, people!" I barked. "Get to your chairs, quick!"

As the clock showed 7:30PM and in time for the downbeat, I stepped to the podium and bowed to the audience.

"Eeek!" came a muffled scream from one of the flutists.

As I turned to see what was the matter there was a roar of laughter from the audience. As my face formed a puzzled look one of the clarinet players wiggled his finger, signaling me to lean over, which produced even more laughter.

"Mr. Olson," whispered the clarinetist, "the right rear of your pants is missing!"

As I turned to look, sure enough, there was a 4-inch square missing from the back of my jeans.

"How did your concert go, last night?" asked Cranky, as he munched his sandwich in the faculty room. "I have been hearing a rumor that it was one of the most entertaining concerts that Lost Hollow has had."

"Let's just say there were some 'holes' in the performance," I replied, "but I was in time for the downbeat!" Smiling, I bit into my buffalo burger.

PRISCILLA PUKSWANKLE

Have you ever met someone new who has had an impact on your life … for good or bad? For a businessperson it could be a customer who makes one of the most major purchases you've ever sold. Or maybe it could be a new friendship that is exciting. For others it could be a despairing event such as a new boss who takes pleasure in creating a new "hell" in your life or a new neighbor who thinks 2 AM is a good time to START a party. For me, Priscilla Pukswankle was someone who trumped all of those situations.

The day that Priscilla arrived at my school was a day that about 700 students, approximately 50 staff, a principal, assistant principal, one custodian, the police department, fire department, 14 dogs and one band director will never forget. That day was a Wednesday in the middle of September. I was in the middle of yelling..er, instructing my 8th grade students on how to play in tune, even though they knew only 5 notes, when Priscilla Pukswankle walked into my class waiving an admit slip from the office.

She was wearing a perfectly clean, white chiffon dress, white shoes (with no scuffs), and a big white bow in her perfectly styled blonde hair. The kids just stared with their mouths open. Tommy Feldman, our tuba player who was known by the monicker, "Blap," asked, "Is it Easter, Mr. Olson?"

"Easter is on a Sunday, Tommy," I responded, frowning.

The blonde girl was holding out a note to me. I took it and read the note, which indicated that this girl "Priscilla", of her OWN volition, wanted to take band. I was surprised at how large the office secretary had written, "OWN VOLITION."

"There must be some mistake," I said confusedly, "I ran out chocolate a week ago. Why do you want to take band?"

"I love music," came the reply.

"Then why have you signed up for my class?" I queried in disbelief. "Never mind that. What instrument do you play?" I asked as I eyed with suspicion a small case in her hands.

As her nose went up 3 inches she smugly said, "I play the flute!"

A gasp came forth from the mouths of most of my band students. There hadn't been anyone who could truly play a flute in the past 8 years at Lost Hollow Middle School and only half the kids who showed up with one could put it together right.

"Right," I chortled. "Do you know how to put it together?" I asked as I gave a sideways knowing look at my students. They all turned their heads to give me the same look back. As I turned back her flute was already put together CORRECTLY! At least I thought it was put together the right way. I saw it once in a book. "Well, can you play something on it? I notice it still has all its pads."

"Sure. What would you like to hear?" She scoffed.

"How about the C Major sca......" No sooner had I begun to say "scale" than she ripped off a three octave C Major Scale up and down with a trill at the top, a cambiata on the bottom, a C Major arpeggio, and a Mozartian type flourish for an ending, all within 1.6 seconds. I don't think my jaw fell off of my face although it might have bounced on the floor. I turned to look at my students and saw 35 jaws bouncing on the floor, including Blap's jaw, whose mouth showed what he had been chewing on during this class period. "You have a cavity in your right back molar, Mr. Olson," indicated Priscilla.

Thinking that I couldn't have possibly heard what I just heard at Lost Hollow Middle School I said, "I'll bet you can't play a chromatic scale more than 3 octaves...."

Have you ever thought about an event in your history where you wished you could have done or said something differently? No sooner had I said "octaves" than Priscilla flew through the chromatic scale at about Mach 2, cruising through the treble clef like an F-16 fighter pilot would cruise straight up through a cumulus cloud, flying through ledger lines, going through notes that I believe are past the right end highest notes of the piano and landing on something so high I couldn't hear it. I know she was playing something up there, though, because of a few things that happened. First, my right lens of my glasses cracked, my office window shattered and the dogs in the adjacent neighborhood started barking and howling. Then Priscilla started coming back down the scale, then up, then down. It was uncanny how much she sounded like our earthquake warning siren….and so loud!

Just before I took my glasses off to see what happened I noticed all the kids were under their chairs hanging onto the back legs. Then I heard the sirens and noticed the barking sounds were closer. I looked out the window and saw a bunch of dogs jumping at the band room door and saw the fire trucks pulling in. I decided I better let the office know what had just happened so I headed down there. On the way I notice all of the students and teachers in the other classes were under their desks. When I got to the office there wasn't anyone there…or at least standing.

"Where's the principal?" I shouted over the din of sirens. "Under here!" came the reply. There was Mr. Togglemeyer, crouched under his desk, which was quite the sight because Mr. T. liked his doughnuts, and was certainly not the smallest man in our school. Before I could say anything five men from the fire department came exploding through the door.

"The alarm indicates this building is on fire!" yelled the captain. "Where is it located?"

Just then I realized that I could still hear Priscilla's flute. I forgot to tell her to stop. As I was thinking that, the sound stopped as if she heard my thoughts. But in place of it came screams, which seemed to be coming from the direction of the band room but getting closer. I poked my head around the office door but drew it back just in time to see Priscilla racing past being chased close behind by a pack of dogs. Too late I saw Ms. Bartolow, the custodian, round the corner heading towards Priscilla. Bartolow didn't have time to scream.

I ran after Priscilla, leaving the fire department to peel Ms. Bartolow off the floor, and found Priscilla outside near the top of the flag pole, still clutching her flute. The dogs were at the base of it, jumping up as if they had treed some wild animal. With a look of compassion I said, "Wow! How were you able to climb that pole with your flute still in your hand?" It amazes me how little some people like scientific questions. Instead of answering me, Priscilla shot a lightning bolt directly out of her left eye socket and hit me right between the eyes. As I staggered over to get the dogs settled down the guys from the fire department came out of the building.

"Are you OK?" one of them asked.

"I'm just a little dazed," I remarked.

"I was talking to the girl!" he retorted.

Months later I was reflecting upon what an asset Priscilla was to our school. She was able to really help us at teacher meetings, which, at our school, were typically just speeches monologued by our principal. At the appropriate time just before the meeting I would have Priscilla practice that special scale, which of course would have us evacuate and so end the meeting. Before Priscilla I never realized how valuable the flute is to the band!

NICKNAMES

Tommy Feldman was a tuba player. That is to say, he held the tuba. Not only did he hold the tuba, but he held it professionally. There have been professional tubists who have come close to being able to hold their tubas as well as Tommy, but I can personally attest to Tommy's tuba holding abilities as being unmatched. Yep, there are few musicians I've known who could hold a tuba better than Blap, which happened to be Tommy's nickname.

These days nicknames are becoming more rare and seldom are they politically correct. But you have to realize that back then, in Lost Hollow, they were as part of everyday life as one would say "car" instead of "automobile" or "fridge" instead of "refrigerator." Because of the Native American influence in our state, nicknames tended to be earned or descriptive instead of just appointed, which is how Blap got his nickname.

I have a tradition on the first day of band of just having kids learn how to open and close their instrument cases. And maybe if they are really perceptive (and complaining), I let them 'hold' their instruments but not play them. This has the effect of postponing the inevitable for at least one day.

"Students," I would say, "when you have learned the fingerings (or slide positions in the case of trombonists) then you get to play the first notes in the book."

"Aww!" would come the collective groan.

"I tell you what," I would declare cheerily, "we'll make this a reward activity. You put your mouthpiece in one of these plastic sandwich bags I am handing out, put your name on it with this marker, and give it to me. As soon as you have proven you know the fingerings of the first five notes I'll let you have your mouthpiece back!"

"Aww!"

"And you percussion players put your names on your sticks and give them to me. When you can play the rhythms for the first page using your hands then I will give you your sticks back."

"Grrr." Drummers have a hard time with "Aww."

I want you to know that I came up with this ingenious approach all by myself, as opposed to most of my other ingenious ideas, which were "borrowed" from John Cranklemeyer, the PE teacher. However, there was one time I didn't follow my own plan. That's because when Tommy Feldman came to beginning band class he already held his tuba like a professional. That's how I think he suckered me into letting him have a mouthpiece.

I remember that fateful day.

That was the day that Tommy broke the two band office windows with only one note. "Tommy," I said as I grabbed his mouthpiece, "It was unfair of me to give you your mouthpiece before having you learn fingerings like the other kids." That mouthpiece ended up in my padlocked mouthpiece drawer. The effect that event had on the future was more than just to keep the window repair guy in work. It also helped create Tommy's nickname, "Blap."

One day Blap had all of the fingerings of the first page memorized and wanted try using his mouthpiece. "You sure you don't want to try memorizing page 2 first?" I asked squeamishly.

"I already memorized it too, Mr. Olson," beamed Tommy.

Well, you cannot believe the amount of howling that was produced when I decided to give Blap his mouthpiece. After I got the percussion players to stop howling I gave Blap the mouthpiece and let him try to play a note. I was amazed at how Blap, with just his tuba, was able to mimic the howling sounds of the percussionists. I don't know if he was ever able to repeat that amazing feat because the next day his mouthpiece came up missing. It was too bad we couldn't get another one out of the mouthpiece drawer because I had lost the key. Of course, the students and I spent an entire class period trying to find Blap's mouthpiece. You would be amazed how quiet a band room can get when kids are trying to find a tuba mouthpiece instead of practicing on their instruments! In fact, I wrote quite a few lesson plans later on that included trying to find that mouthpiece. Bless Blap's heart. He sure could hold a tuba well though.

There were other nicknames with which some of my students were tagged. Jimmy Thornbush was named "Crow". He played the trumpet. Then there was Vanity Parkowicz. The students liked calling her "Elephant." She wasn't big and, in fact, was fairly skinny. But when she played her French Horn she had the ability of transporting you into an African forest or the Woodland Park Zoo. In fact, I remember at the end of one of our concerts one of the parents came up to me complimenting us on the "African number." That was Tchaikovsky's "Nutcracker Suite." My students know how to put their own "character" in a piece.

The nickname given to drummer, David Putnum was "Sticks." Duh.

A few other nicknames were "Foghorn," given to Lisa Dearborn, the baritone saxophonist; "Ducky," who was oboist Bobbie Crandall; and "Misfire," the trombonist Mickey Fenton. Mickey, when warming up, sounded a lot like my car engine. Speaking of cars, I am reminded of Jack Packwood, who tried to play the alto saxophone. Unfortunately, Jack could never quite get the control of that mouthpiece and would squeal and squeak uncontrollably, perfectly resembling either the brakes on my car. I understand he got a job later on for a sound effects company in Hollywood. Anyway, Jack's nickname was "Brakes." He had a special talent.

There was also Barney Wertelmeyer. Barney started with the nickname: "The Pest". Personally, I felt that the band students (and most of the school) were quite unfair to use that nickname for Barney so I banned its use. I felt that "Ragweed" was much more appropriate. I had coined that name for Ragw... er, Barney after I started having acute cases of asthma whenever he would start putting together his instrument. Barney had the uncanny ability to being able to put me onto an inhaler in less than 60 seconds of playing his instrument. He was able to do that with an instrument called the clarinet.

Ragweed also was kind of a behavioral scientist. He experimented with sounds to create a condition called the Daymare (which is not much different than a nightmare). After just a few notes on his clarinet, Ragweed would be able to induce a trance-like state on all of the students, where grotesque facial expressions, wide eyes, and fainting could be observed. Somehow I was not affected that way. My wheezing and palpitations helped me to decide that Ragweed would sound much better without the use of a reed.

I remember a time when Ragweed showed up without his instrument.

"Where's your clarinet, Barney?" I inquired.

"It's on the roof of the school, Mr. Olson," replied Ragweed, rather forlornly.

I looked around the room and saw all the smiles.

"All right," I warned irately, "which one of you threw it on the roof?"

"None of us," said Crow. "Mr. Cranklemeyer threw it up there."

"And just why would he do that?" I asked, looking at Ragweed.

Barney squirmed a little as he responded with, "At the basketball game last night the buzzer wouldn't work on time clock so I tried to make a buzzing sound with my clarinet. I guess I was a little to close to his right ear."

I stood there with my mouth open. Usually, to get Cranky to do something positive like throwing Ragweed's clarinet on the roof, I had to pay him money or loan my guitar to him.

"That is terrible," I sympathized, trying to stifle a chuckle. "The only way to get up there is to get the fire department to bring their big ladder. Maybe we can get that done in a month or two." I chuckled into my hand.

"That's OK, Mr. Olson," countered Ragweed, "my dad works for the fire department and he said he can get it after school."

"Oh," I groaned.

"Oh," the class groaned.

One day Ragweed was trying to pester the band by practicing what he called a scale warm up. But the kids in the band knew better. They knew Ragweed was just trying to make everyone have daymares and to start up my asthma. This is where Blap became a school-wide hero. Blap was ready to haul off and turn Ragweed into Canadian bacon when I cautioned him about the fact we don't allow food in the band room. As I was walking into my office to get my inhaler I noticed the daymare sounds had stopped. I also noticed Ragweed was not to be seen.

"Bla...er, Tommy! Where is Ragw... er, Barney?" I barked. Blap, who was leaning on his inverted tuba simply said, "I think he had to go to the bathroom." At that moment the bell rang and the 6th grade band was over for the day. Blap put his tuba away into his case while the rest of the class also put away their instruments.

I had two more classes that day. But I couldn't quite get the sound of Ragweed's daymares out of my head. For the next two hours I kept thinking I heard the sound of Ragweed's clarinet coming out of the instrument storage room.

On the way home I bought an extra inhaler.

HELP! I'M IN THE BAND!

There have been many famous people in history who have overcome great challenges on their way to success. Some who come to mind are Abraham Lincoln, George Washington, Winston Churchill, Dwight D. Eisenhower, and Greg Olson. All of those names are very recognizable to me, especially the last one. That happens to be my name.

Now, I can imagine that some might be offended at my name being mentioned in context with those other prestigious names. Some might be offended at the mentioning of my name by itself. But if you hear my story you might feel a little more empathetic, and that is a sight better than pathetic, which would describe the state of my life at one point. You see, this is the story of a great challenge. I was placed in charge of the Lost Hollow BAND! Did you notice I said placed? It was not by willingness that I became Lost Hollow's Band Director. Here's what happened.

I was minding my own business, reading over the newspaper in the teacher's lunchroom, instead of reading over my students' papers from my U.S. History class. I felt that keeping abreast of the current events was much better for my indigestion than reading 30 papers that had more misspellings than John Cranklemeyer's dog has fleas. John was the Physical Education teacher at Lost Hollow School, a good friend, and someone who was willing to banter with me at lunch.

"I thought you said you were going to read over those term papers from your history class during lunch, today," inquired Cranky, which was John's nickname.

"It was a little difficult to digest them," I countered.

Cranky laughed. "What's so hard about digesting 10th grade history papers?"

"I was talking about digesting my hard boiled eggs," I said, frowning. "Reading those papers always upsets my appetite. Besides, I'm beginning to think that I'm not cut out for this kind of vocation. I am just not one who enjoys paperwork."

"Then you might be interested in the new proposal by the school board."

"What proposal?" I asked, while trying to stab a hardboiled egg. My wife, Darla, was under the impression that if a fork could pierce a hardboiled egg it was not yet done. The positive side to this philosophy was that no one ever stole my lunch.

"The school board has decided to start a band class at Lost Hollow," Cranky said, as he dumped about a fourth of the shaker of salt into his soup.

"And why would that interest me?" I inquired while raising one eyebrow and stabbing at my egg. Raising two eyebrows would be indicating a sincere interest, which I was not yet ready to do.

"Don't you see?" he replied. "There's no paperwork if you are teaching a band class. And since you are a musician......"

"Whoa, whoa," I cried. "I just play guitar. I don't know anything about band instruments!"

"How hard can it be? I have a buddy down at Arrowhead that teaches band. He says the kids have a book that shows how to hold their instruments, how to get sounds, and all the fingerings. All you have to do is make them read it. That's gotta be as easy as spearing a hardboiled egg!"

"Hmm," I expounded, raising two eyebrows. "There could be some potential here." I stabbed at my hardboiled egg, again, pitching it into Cranky's soup.

The next day, while my 9th grade students were taking a chapter test on Washington State History, Mrs. Stubbleberg, the principal walked into my class.

"Greg," she whispered, "could I see you before you go to lunch, today?"

"Sur… sure," I stammered, trying to place what I did this time to get in trouble. Let's see, I hadn't done the paper airplane wars, yet. That always worked for the Blitzkrieg Battles. We hadn't catapulted mud-bombs at farmer Schmidt's pigs to demonstrate the Crusades strategy. I was at a loss to understand what was my offense.

"Well, Greg, I understand you are interested in the new band job that just opened up," Mrs. Stubbleberg began, while closing the door to her office.

I stood there with my mouth opened, trying to comprehend how she came to that conclusion. The only person I talked to about that was Cranky. Cranky! News sure travels fast in a school.

"News travels pretty fast in a school!" she continued. "John Cranklemeyer says that you are looking into the job."

"I thought it might be possibility," I replied, a little flabbergasted.

"Really, Greg? I thought you would be leaping for this opportunity. This would be right down your alley. It's so hard to get a good music teacher to come to these small out-of-the-way towns and this would probably be a good fit for you. There is very little paperwork which might give you a little more time for fishing."

"Well…."

"Great!" she exclaimed. "I'll send the transfer paperwork down to your room. Now, I'm sorry to have to do this to you, Greg, but I have a meeting right now down at the administration building. See you later!" With that she was out the door.

As I stood there staring at the door, I realized I never even got to sit down.

At lunchtime I walked into the faculty room to hear applause and "Congratulations!" from the staff. As they watched me come through the door they were clapping and saying things like, "We finally get a band in Lost Hollow!" and "Music in our school, yeah!" and "Way to support the school, Greg!" and finally, "Good luck with the beginning band!"

Not only was that last comment was a little unnerving, but the speed of rumor in that school was something akin to the speed of light. Still, I relished all of the attention.

"I heard that Billy Middleton is doing drums," Cranky said, smiling the kind of smile a wolverine might give to a squirrel. Billy had been sent home from Lost Hollow Middle School for behavior problems more times than some kids showed up for school.

"M..Maybe he might be good at drums," I groaned. A chorus of laughter went around the room. Unfortunately, this chorus was not the kind of musical performance that I eagerly anticipated.

The beginning of the following school year was full of excitement. Kids were excited about seeing all of their friends. Teachers were excited about a new batch of students. I was excited about the fact I couldn't find my earplugs.

"What are you rifling through that drawer for?" asked Cranky, who was impatiently waiting for me so he could drive us down to the school.

"I can't find my earplugs!" I hollered out of my bedroom.

Cranky laughed. "It's NOT going to be that bad, Greg!"

As I stepped out of my bedroom I asked, "Do you think this will work?"

Cranky roared with laughter. "With those tissues sticking out of your ears, you look like something from outer space!"

"Oh, well," I replied, while pulling the tissues from my ears. "If I go deaf it might be a GOOD thing."

As the day went on, I realized that ALL of the bands, no matter what grade level, were beginning groups and that I would be hearing the same noises all day long. I think there is something written in the Geneva Convention code for prisoners that outlaws that kind of torture. I somehow survived the first four class periods of band. Maybe that's because we actually don't use the instruments on the first day of class. When the final class of the day strolled in, there was Billy Middleton, truckin' in with them. Billy doesn't stroll, he trucks, which is probably his way of stating, "I am here because I feel like it, and you should be honored that I showed up!"

As Billy came in, I noticed the weapon in his hand. "Billy!" I cried. "What do you think you are going to do with THAT!" I exclaimed, pointing at his right hand.

"These are drum sticks, Mr. Olson. I'm going to play drums!"

"Oh", I replied, sheepishly, remembering that my retirement was not for another 20 years.

The first few days of band were spent showing the students how to hold the instruments, how to produce a sound, and how to make the different notes. If you had walked into the band room in those days you would have heard the following dialogue:

"Mr. Olson, how do I hold my clarinet?"

"Page 2 in the book."

"Mr. Olson, how do I make a sound on my trumpet?"

"Page 3 in the book."

"Mr. Olson, how do I finger the note 'F'?"

"Look in the back of the book, Charmagne."

And so on. My last class period was a little different than the other classes. You would have heard more specific comments:

"Billy, I think you will get a better drum sound if you don't raise your sticks higher than your head when hitting the drum."

"Billy, the bass drum sounds better without the pencil holes in it."

"Billy, when the music has a rest, it doesn't mean take a nap."

And, "Billy, if you let go of Bob's neck and use two hands, your drum-roll will sound smoother."

I could always tell when Billy wasn't in class because of the disappointment heard in the other kid's voices. Some might mistake those sounds as cheering. And when people like Bob and Jimmy would come up and ask if we could have a party, I knew they were just trying to disguise their regret in missing one of their musical teammates. Still, the class seemed to move a little faster on the non-Billy days.

For the next month, Billy missed half the school days. On the days he was forced to come someone would make crank phone calls to the school office. The calls would sound something like this: "Help! The school's on fire!" or "The dam has busted and there is a wall of water heading right for Lost Hollow Middle School!" and "Help! There is a tornado heading right for the school!" I have to admit, Billy's alarms got more and more creative, while he tried to get school dismissed. But, after a while, the secretaries began recognizing Billy's voice.

"Sorry, Billy, you'll have to do better than that to get out of school today."

"Aw, shucks," would be the response.

One day at lunch, Cranky had asked if I had kicked Billy out of band class, yet.

"He usually doesn't set fire to your room 'till about December, when it gets fairly cold."

Alarmed, I replied, "What makes him do those things?"

"Billy's father sees school as an intrusion into his son's chores of slopping the hogs or feeding the cattle. Maybe that's why Billy's father was kicked out of school when he was a kid."

When Cranky began filling me in on Billy's home life or lack thereof, I began to feel guilty about my pleasure in missing one of my students. The principal had indicated that half of those missed days were because Billy was suspended for fighting or setting fires in the boy's bathroom. The other half he just chose not to come to school or couldn't get a ride.

"The bus driver doesn't let him on the bus anymore," the principal had mentioned.

When I found out that he lived just a little ways off of the road that I took to school, I decided one morning to drop by and see if he needed a ride. Back in those days it wasn't taboo to give a kid a lift.

I walked up to the door to knock. I assumed it was a door because there was a 6-foot rectangular hole in the front of the house covered by a piece of plywood. I knocked. There was no sound. I knocked louder. Still nothing. I banged on the plywood with my fist and for a moment I thought I heard movement but then nothing. I noticed a crow bar lying about fifteen feet away underneath one of the 3 junk cars in the front yard. I used it to bang on the piece of plywood.

"What's goin' on!" I heard from somewhere inside the house.

After about a minute I heard from the other side of the door, "Who's there!"

It was Billy's voice. "It's Mr. Olson, Billy. I stopped by to see if you need a ride to school."

There was silence for a moment and then, "Would you mind repeatin' what you just said, Mr. Olson?"

"Yeah, Billy, I'm just checking to see if you need a lift."

"Back away."

"Come on, Billy. I drove out of my way come and get you."

"Naw, Mr. Olson, I meant back away from the door."

I moved back, then all of a sudden the plywood door fell forward and there was Billy, rubbing the sleep out of his eyes. "Ya really came here ta pick me up?" He exclaimed, yawning.

On the way to school, I noticed out the corner of my eye that Billy kept staring at me.

"Is there some egg on my face, Billy?"

"I don't see any, Mr. Olson. Why'd ya ask?"

"Because you keep staring at me, Billy."

"I'm just amazed that you would drive me to school, Mr. Olson."

"It's no big deal, Billy. Your house is pretty much on my way to school."

We arrived at school and we both headed off towards our first period classes. That day, two things surprised me. First was that Billy made it all the way to 7th period without behind kicked out of school. The second was his response to my encouragement.

"Billy, would you mind letting go of Jonathan's arm? He'll probably play the drum better with his arm in front of his body."

"Sure, Mr. Olson. Whatever you say!"

The class went silent. I was speechless. Jonathan, with his arm released, stayed in the position with his arm behind him.......just in case Billy might change his mind.

"Er, uh, thanks, Billy."

As soon as the rest of the drummers got out from underneath their chairs we continued the class, which was uneventful for the rest of the period.

I dropped Billy off at his house and said, "I'll pick you up at 8 o'clock sharp tomorrow, Billy."

"Really? Well, ok Mr. Olson. I'll be ready."

For the next two months Billy set a record for the number of days he actually attended school. My percussionists even stopped flinching when he grabbed his drumsticks. We all flinched, though, when he grabbed the crash cymbals. Finesse wasn't Billy's strong suit.

Finally, it was time for the annual Band Festival, which was to be held down at Arrowhead this year. All the band kids got their instruments and music and then boarded the bus. As we headed towards Arrowhead, the bus driver reminded me that the best way to Arrowhead was logging road 4301.

"Otherwise, you have to add two hours each way!" he croaked.

I did not relish spending an extra four hours on the bus with my students so I said, "Whatever you think is best."

To my eyes, Logging Road 4301 did not look like a highway, roadway, or even a trail.

"Watch out for that sink-hole!" I exclaimed.

The driver laughed. "What? That little pothole? The sink-hole isn't fer another mile!"

As the bus wove in between pot-holes, branches, tree stumps, I began thinking about my will and how outdated it was. Suddenly, the bus slid to a stop. Looking out the front window I noticed that the road was gone.

"Looks like the road was washed out," observed the bus driver. It was obvious that there was no way past.

"How are we going to turn around?" I asked, in exasperation.

"There was a side road about 4 miles back," said the driver. "I'll just have to back up to it. You can help me by going to the back of the bus and give me directions over those potholes and stumps."

"No! Right, I said!" I yelled, as the bus careened around a four-foot wide stump. I had to remember that my right was the bus driver's left when going backwards. "Do you have to go this fast?!"

Just then I saw us heading on a collision-course to the mother-of-all-boulders.

"Left, quick!" I screamed, but then realized should have said "right" because of being in reverse. "Wait! Go right!" The bus barely careened off that boulder, heading towards the edge of the road. That wasn't much of a big deal, except for the thousand-foot drop-off. We all screamed. If there was ever a competition for speed praying I think I would have earned a Gold Medal right then and there.

The bus slipped off the embankment and began its downward plummet. In less than two seconds it stopped. I slowly opened one eye to see a beautiful cloud floating about 300 yards away and 100 yards below us.

"Don't anybody move!" came the shout from the bus driver.

"How come we're not falling?" I exclaimed.

"We are centered on a tree, Mr. Olson. We are perfectly balanced, which is why nobody can move. If any weight is shifted forward or back, we'll go straight down the cliff!"

"What'll we do?" Charmagne began to cry.

"We need the person sitting in the middle seat, where the emergency door is, to bust out and go get help."

The fear on everyone's face intensified ten-fold as we saw who that person was. Billy was already working the emergency door open. The bus creaked.

"Slowly, son, slowly!" croaked the bus driver.

Billy clambered out and was able to scamper up the ten feet to the road.

"Don't worry, Mr. Olson, I'll get help!" he yelled. Instead, of heading down the road, he started going up the hill.

"Where are you going?" I exclaimed.

"I know a short-cut to the ranger station," came the reply. In another minute he was into the trees and gone. Thinking that he might not be the right person for the job, I began to get up and move toward the emergency door. The bus began to creak and I froze.

"Sit down!" the bus driver yelled, angrily. I sat.

From various accounts I was able to piece together what happened after Billy left. When he got to the ranger station it was closed but there was an emergency phone outside. He dialed the one number he had memorized.

"Lost Hollow Middle School," came the response from inside the phone. "Mrs. Smith speaking."

"Help! I'm in the band!" Billy shouted into the phone.

The secretary recognized Billy's voice.

"I'm sorry, Billy, it's not going to work this time. Although, I have not heard you use that one before."

"No, really!" he exasperated. "The bus went off a cliff and I'm the only one who got out and...."

The laughter coming from the receiver was loud and non-ending.

"Please, please!" Billy exclaimed.

But the howling from the other end never ceased. Billy slammed the phone down.

"How long do you think it will take him to get to the ranger station?" I asked of the driver.

"It would take about 2 hours if he was to take the road, but he said he knew a short cut" the bus driver responded. "Is he the kind of kid you can count on?" There was an instant roar of laughter and crying all at the same time. With a miserable expression I thought, "I hope so," as I looked at another cloud floating by.

Eventually it started to get dark. Most of the kids had fallen asleep. All of a sudden I heard a distant rumbling of a motor. I could also feel the vibration of some large vehicle. The tree could feel that same vibration because it began to creak as its roots started loosening their hold of the ground. The bus dropped about a foot. There were screams.

"Don't anybody move!" yelled the bus driver.

As the big rig lumbered forth I saw that it was one of those yarders, a big contraption with cables that loggers would use to move downed trees to the road. The movement, however, caused more vibration, allowing more of the tree roots to give way. We dropped another foot amid screams and wailing. One of the bright scientific kids let us all know that we would plummet a thousand feet if our tree didn't hold. This, of course, caused more crying and wailing, along with some dirty looks from the driver and band teacher.

Finally, the yarder was right above us. Some men, bringing cables, were attaching them underneath the front and rear of the bus. And there was Billy, standing on the road with a big grin on his face. We could hear the metallic clanks underneath the bus as the men attached their cables. All of a sudden, amidst a loud creaking, the tree completely gave way, sending us to our death……..(just kidding). The cables held, causing us to drop only about half a foot. The yarder began hauling us up, inch-by-inch. When the bus was completely on the road the kids were cheering, the driver was mopping his forehead with a hanky, and was praying his thanks. The kids piled off the bus and when they saw Billy, they gave a big cheer with lots of pats on the back. The embarrassed Billy dropped his head with a few "Aw, shucks."

When I asked Billy how he got the school to send help so fast, he mentioned that he decided to use a different source.

"My uncle Marvin is a logging foreman and he just lives four miles from here. He's the one that got his crew to come out to help us."

My favorite class for the rest of the year was Billy's class. It had the best discipline. Kids that tended to be distracting or talk out of turn were usually treated to one of Billy's "flame-thrower" looks and that would do the trick. Billy also learned how to play a two-handed drum roll and I learned how to read band music, which is a good thing since I signed on to be the band teacher for another year.

WATER KEYS

These days, having to be Politically Correct, or P.C., is more obvious than ever before. One can come to this conclusion by looking at today's schoolbooks. Method books in band are no different than other books as is evidenced by the two words: water keys. You see, when I was a child in band class everybody called them spit valves. A spit valve…excuse me… water key is necessary on many wind instruments because of the interaction of the human body and the instrument when it is played. When a person "blows" into an instrument the air comes out of the lungs. Along with the air comes moisture, which collects along the inner walls of the instrument as miniature droplets. As these droplets join together they begin to collect in certain areas inside the instrument and if the tubing is small enough, this can produce a "gurgling" sound. This sound is usually a detractor from a quality performance unless you happen to be Tommy Feldman, in which case the gurgling sound could actually be one of the best sounds coming out of your tuba.

As I said before, the PC way of referring to this device is the water key. However, when one has used the old descriptor for this gizmo for many years it is easy to slip back into old habits to the chagrin of some of my students. Near the start of the year one of my lessons is to teach about the use of this water key to my beginning band class.

This is such an important lesson that the principal, custodian and nurse have it listed on their personal calendars. What amazes me is the fact that the three of them are almost always missing from school on that day. There was one time, however, that the custodian, Ms. Bartolow, was not gone on that day. "Ms. Bartolow," I wondered, "usually you are gone on the day I teach about the water key.

"Oh my gosh," she said in astonishment, "this can't be the day you teach that!"

"Of course!" I chaffed, "I always teach it on the Tuesday of the 2nd week of September."

"2nd week? I thought this was the 3rd week!" said Ms. Bartolow agitatedly and started sweating and looking side to side as if to escape.

Noticing her somewhat agitated state I said, " Ms. Bartolow, you don't have to worry. I made a couple of improvements to my lesson plan so it shouldn't be so messy. By the way, where are you going?"

"I have to alert the nurse's substitute and the acting principal since the regular ones stayed home today. I might also call the Fire Department."

I never knew that Ms. Bartolow could move that fast.

"Class," I monotoned, "I would like to show you how to use a spit valve."

I love to look at the expressions of the clarinet section after that is said. Looks of disgust to downright horror pervade their faces. "You see, the spit val...."

"Mr. Olson, the book calls it a water key."

"Right you are, Priscilla," I intoned. Priscilla was the first chair flutist and piccolo player in our band. But more importantly, she was the P.C. monitor for our entire school. Self-appointed, of course.

"The water key is used to empty the spi.... er...water from your instruments." More faces and now groans from the clarinet section. Clarinets don't have a water key. In fact, most woodwinds don't have one because the design of those instruments makes it unnecessary. To compete with the brass water key, clarinets and saxophones have the five-month-old, bacteria-infested, moldy 'reed'. Some of the more health-conscious reed players will change them more often but that makes for less interesting stories and facial expressions.

"One of my older students, Tommy, has come here from another class to help demonstrate how to use the water key," I explained, smiling. "Let's look at Tommy's tuba and see his spit, I mean, water key on the main tubing pipe. Tommy, when was the last time you used this, uh, water key?"

"Gosh, Mr. Olson, I forgot I had one."

The groans from the clarinets had begun increasing in volume and frequency.

"Well, Tommy, maybe that's why your sounds aren't always what a tuba player's sounds should be! I tell you what, just to be safe let's use this garbage receptacle over here."

The wailing coming now from the clarinets is some of the best sound I have ever had from this section. Too bad they weren't using their clarinets to make those sounds.

"Tommy, hold your tuba over the garbage can and depress that water key."

"You mean like this, Mr. Ols..."

I lost the last part of Tommy's question in the caterwailing that proceeded not only from the clarinets but just about the entire band as Tommy let forth a stream that brought to one's mind images of Niagara, Victoria, Bridal Veil, and the like. As I turned away I saw Priscilla jump up and race past Tommy and me, heading for the door. I am not sure if she was more shocked at Tommy's work or the greenish pallor on my face but she had managed to knock over Tommy's garbage can on her way out. As if on cue, the entire class pointed to the mess on the floor, let out one unified groan and within 30 seconds not one student except Tommy was left in the room.

"Wow, Mr. Olson! That was cool! That was almost as cool as when Sam brought the principal's coffee cup to the garbage dumpster and we...."

"Well, Tommy, I guess that finishes today's lesson," I gasped. "You can go back to your regular class, now."

"OK, Mr. Olson," Tommy beamed. "Thanks for letting me demonstrate."

I was reaching for my phone to call the custodian when it rang. It was the acting principal.

"Mr. Olson, would you mind coming down here to the nurse's room? It seems 15 of your students are heading home because of illness. Do you think there might be something wrong with the water in your room?"

I didn't have the stomach to tell him.

BAND SAVES DAM

There are some rare moments in one's life where the truly unexpected bonanza rolls in. Today was one of those moments. Sitting at my table was my lovely wife, Darla. Any time Darla was not hounding me with the "honey-do" list I considered her lovely. Also, there were six others with us. My cronies, Cranky Cranklemeyer and Tom Brandston were also seated at our table along with Darla's parents and sisters. The table next to us contained eight of my in-laws. I didn't know that I had so many relatives. I actually didn't find out I had that many relatives until it was announced in the Lost Hollow Gazette that I was one of ten finalists for the 85 million dollar drawing that was to take place in the next ten minutes.

"Ladies and Gentlemen: Don't leave your seats. The drawing will take place precisely at 8:00!"

I took my eyes off the emcee and glanced at my watch, which indicated 7:50 PM. In ten minutes I was to find out if I was a multimillionaire. But I had already decided to just be cool and collected seeing as how the odds of me winning was ten to one against me.

"Wow, Greg. You sure are sweating! Gettin' nervous?" posed Cranky.

"I'm not getting nervous!" I retorted as I wiped my forehead with my second hanky. The first one was soaked. "It just happens to be kinda warm in here."

"You've got to be kidding." quipped Darla, who was wearing about five layers of clothing. "I just asked them to turn up the heat."

I looked over at the "in-law" table and noticed all of those people smiling and bobbing their heads at me, not unlike those bobble-head dolls the Seattle Mariners give out to increase their odds; not the odds of winning, just the odds of making a profit. Trying to effect the odds of winning was obviously set aside for some future date. But I digress.

"And now the drawing!" shouted the emcee.

"You sure look nervous," stated Tom.

"I always get nervous when I hear a drum roll," I snapped.

"Then stop drumming the table with your fingers!" I drew back my hand as I looked up at the announcer.

"And the winner is......," stated the emcee as he reached into a hat containing ten name cards.

"..... the winner is Greg Olson!"

I was speechless. That was probably because my jaw had settled somewhere between my dinner plate and my water glass. My table erupted into loud cheering and clapping, which was only upstaged by the loud cheering and clapping created by the "in-laws" table.

"Greg Olson, come on down! You have 60 seconds to come down and claim your prize!"

As I tried to rise, I noticed that my legs didn't work. As hard as I tied to stand, I found out I couldn't move.

Cranky said, "Get up, Greg!" Tom said, "Get up, Greg!" The in-law table said in one unison voice, "Get up, Greg!"

"30 seconds!"

Darla started shaking me. "Wake up, you fool! Time's running out!"

But I couldn't stand.

"15 seconds!"

Cranky started shaking me, too. "Wake up, Greg. Wake up!" And I did.

I opened my eyes to see the back of the bus driver's head. Mrs. Carlson was shaking me while exclaiming, "Wake up, Greg! We're here."

I looked out the window to see the newly built Stagomish River Dam looming just ahead.

"No, no! Let me go back to sleep. I won! I won!" I exclaimed as I tried to close my eyes.

"Oh no you don't," laughed Mrs. Carlson as she shook me again. "You've got get these kids ready to play!"

I turned in my seat to see 45 of the finest musicians on this bus. Of course, there WERE only 45 kids on the bus, so that would make them the "finest"…..or the worst, but I preferred to look at the cup half full. Today was the dedication of the dam, and the Lost Hollow High School Band, under the direction of Greg Olson, yours truly, was scheduled to perform at this event.

As the kids piled out of the bus, I made sure to snag Tommy, our star tuba player. "Blap," I called, "make sure you and your brother don't warm up at the same time."

"I know, Mr. Olson. Timmy and I have a warm-up schedule worked out."

Timmy (a.k.a. Blurp), who was Tommy's younger brother, was also the other half of the tuba "duel" in our band. Some of you more savvy musician types probably think I meant to say "duo" instead of "duel." I didn't. You see, Blap and Blurp were two of the loudest tuba players in Whatcom county, and the state of Washington, and quite possibly the United States of America. The only problem with these two boys is that they rarely played in tune.

As Timmy was waiting to get his tuba off the bus he said, "Mr. Olson, how come you don't let Tommy and me warm up at the same time?" That prompted the memory of that first day that the band played this year. I remember hearing a freight train bearing down on the band room, only to discover that it was just Blap, …er Tommy Feldman, warming up his tuba. But when Timmy (Blurp), his brother, also started warming up his tuba, three things happened:

All the kids in the room found themselves under their chairs, hanging onto two of the chair legs, the walls of the room started shaking at about 7.6 on the Richter scale, and the earthquake warning alarm started going off.

In answer to his question, I said, "Timmy, it's important that the other kids can actually hear themselves when they warm up."

As I was speaking to Blurp, a young lady who was dressed as though she was going to sell me some perfume at the local mall walked up to me with a wide smile and said, "You must be Mr. Olson, the band director," as she put out her hand. "I'm Jenny." With her other hand she indicated a temporarily constructed small set of bleachers overlooking Steelhead Canyon and Stagomish River Dam, where was perched our mayor and some of the town council. "We have some chairs for your kids placed over there, facing the bleachers. The ceremony will start in about 30 minutes. We are looking forward to hearing your band!"

I smiled and said, "We'll be ready." As I watched her try to walk across the field in those high heels I was hoping I hadn't just lied to her.

I rounded up the kids and we headed over to the staging area hauling our instruments, music, stands, and wearing an interesting hodge-podge of uniforms.

I looked at Barney (alias Ragweed) and said, "How come you're wearing a dress, Barney?"

Ragweed scowled as he said, "This was the smallest coat that you had, Mr. Olson."

Ragweed certainly was the smallest kid in the band. We had bought these used uniforms from the Anacortes band when they purchased their new ones. Unfortunately, they didn't have every size we needed.

The kids found their seats and started warming up. Since I love listening to them warm up as much as I love standing under a falling tree, I decided to find the "high heel" lady, Jenny, and discuss the timing of when we were supposed to play. As Jenny and I were discussing the order of the program, we heard the loud blast of a ferry boat.

"Funny," said Jenny, "I didn't think the ferry boats came up the river."

"They don't!" I yelled, as I began running toward the band. While running as fast as I could I screamed at the band, "That's enough warming up! Don't play anymo……" The last part of my sentence was drowned out by the sound of either ten freight trains, six ferry boats, or two tuba players, and you can guess which it was. As I saw Blap taking a breath for one more blast, I dove at him for a mid-air tackle that I'm sure would have made a Seahawks linebacker jealous. As I picked myself off the ground, I noticed that Blap hadn't even budged an inch. He WAS a big boy.

"Oh hi, Mr. Olson. How come you're lying on the ground? I don't think you have time for a nap……"

"Blap," I squeaked, trying to get the air back in my lungs, "I TOLD you and Blurp not to warm up at the same time!"

"It was my fault, Mr. Olson," said Timmy. "Ragweed said Tommy was louder than me, so I was trying to prove him wrong."

As I glowered at Barney (Ragweed), who was doing a good job of hiding inside his oversized uniform, I said, "Well, it looks like there was no damage." But I spoke too soon. Priscilla, our principal flutist, was pointing a pile of wood and said, "Isn't that where the bleachers were, Mr. Olson?" As I forlornly peered at the disheveled mess, I noticed movement in the middle of the pile. The first thing I saw was the bald head of Mayor Eriksson poking up from the pile. I was wondering where the perfume-sales lady was. I was wondering if I would have a job after today. I was wondering......

"Mr. Olson!" screamed Priscilla. "Look!"

My eyes followed the line of Priscilla's index finger and noticed a small stream of water propelled out from the down-river side of the dam. We all ran onto the dam and looked down to see the stream shooting straight out from about ten feet down the side. I turned and ran to the upstream side where the surface of the water was only about three feet below where we were standing. All of a sudden a man, wearing a Whatcom Power System uniform, ran up next to us and exclaimed, "The temporary valve plug has disintegrated! How could that happen?"

We all turned to stare at Blap and Blurp, who, at that moment, decided to stare at their feet, probably to make sure they were still attached to their bodies.

"If that hole isn't plugged within a few minutes, the water pressure is going to start to widen it!" shouted the uniformed man. "But I don't have anything to plug it with."

I wanted to plug it with Ragweed's head. However, turning to look at the band, I spotted Billy Middleton, one of the drummers. "Billy!" I yelled. "Run quick and bring me your percussion bag!" I shouted to the Power System guy, "Do you have any rope?"

"Sure, but...."

"Just get me some rope, NOW!" The man ran off as I saw Billy running up with his percussion bag. I opened it up and saw what I was looking for, a bass drum mallet. As I held it up to see how thick it was, Billy asked, "What are you going to do with that?!"

"We need a brave volunteer to be lowered into the water and stuff this mallet into the hole."

As I turned to look at the band members I was aware of how many of them were looking down, also trying to find out if THEIR feet were attached to their bodies. Blap came up to me and said, "I should go, Mr. Olson, seeing as how me & my bother caused this thing."

"Blap, I appreciate your bravery, but you are just too heavy for us to lower you," I said as I eyed Ragweed. "Ragweed, your taunting of the tuba players got us into this mess and now is your chance to get us out."

The shrinking clarinet player said, "Su..Sure, Mr. Olson. What can I do?"

"How long can you hold your breath?"

"I uh….." But just then, the Power System man ran up with about 100 feet of rope.

"Alright, Ragweed," I barked. "We're going to tie one end of this rope around your ankle and lower you into the water. You're going to stuff this mallet into that hole."

"But, but, but I can't swim, Mr. Olson!" exclaimed Ragweed, as he started back-pedaling.

"You won't need to swim because we'll have this rope tied to you."

As Ragweed looked down, Billy had already tied the rope around Ragweed's ankle.

"But, but, but….."

"Just remember, Ragweed," I shouted, as I handed him the mallet, "take a big breath, and when we lower you into the water stuff this here mallet into the hole."

When Ragweed was a few inches above the surface of the water I asked, "Are you ready, Ragweed?"

"Su…sure."

"OK. Take a big breath NOW!"

As Ragweed sucked in a big gulp of air, we dropped him into the water. I saw him stuff the mallet into the hole and yelled, Bring him up!"

As the sputtering clarinet player was brought up over the edge, I ran to the other side of the dam in time to see a projectile in the shape of a bass drum mallet sailing through the air like a mini-javelin. The mallet was too small for the hole!

In desperation I ran to Billy's percussion bag and found something else, a couple of cowbells. As I grabbed the smaller of the two, I turned to see something that looked like a drowned rat staring at me. I squatted down and took the rope off the drowned rat. It was obvious that he was in no shape to try to plug the hole again.

As I started tying the rope around my ankle I shouted, "Tommy and Timmy, when I'm done putting this here cowbell into the hole you two will have to haul me up!" I handed them the other end of the rope, took a big breath and jumped into the water.

Finding the hole, I began cramming the cowbell into it but realized that the cowbell was a bit too small. It went in a ways but wasn't wide enough to completely block the hole. As I broke the surface of the water, Blap said, "Should we haul you up, Mr. Olson?"

"No, no! Give me the bigger cowbell!"

The noise of the dam must have been pretty loud because Blap asked, "What?"

"Give me the bigger cowbell!" I yelled.

"What?!"

"MORE COWBELL!!" I screamed.

Time stood still, people smiled at me, and Blap said, "I don't think we have time for kidding around, Mr. Olson." Chuckle, chuckle.

"I think he means he wants the bigger cowbell," said Billy, as he reached into the bag. "Here you go, Mr. Olson," he said as he dropped it into my hands.

As I crammed it into the hole it fit perfectly, completely blocking the flow of the water.

Everybody started cheering and dancing around. Everybody except me, that is. Instead, I said, "W-would y-y-you m-mind p-p-pulling m-me out of th-this c-c-cold water?!

As Blap hauled me up, I saw the mayor heading our way.

"Ragweed exclaimed, "Wow! How does he make steam come out of his ears like that!"

"OLSON!" he roared, as he began to reach for me with his two claws.

He was unable to grab me because at that moment I was hoisted up onto the shoulders of the Power System man and his co-workers.

"You saved the dam, Mr. Olson!" yelled the Power System man amidst cheering by his colleagues and my students.

At that moment a flash went off and there was a photographer from the Gazette standing there along with a reporter.

The reporter shoved a microphone in front of me and asked, "Is it true that you saved the dam, Mr. Olson?"

As I looked at the beaming faces of my students I replied, "Actually, the band saved the dam." A cheer went up from the kids and I didn't feel the need elaborate to the reporter what caused the problem in the first place.

"What do you say to that, Mayor?" asked the reporter as he shoved the mic into the mayor's face.

"Well......," he began, while looking at all of the expectant band students, "we, uh, are very fortunate to have an extremely talented band!" Another cheer went up from the band.

The next morning down at Mable's Café Tom Brandston was holding up the front page of the Lost Hollow Gazette. "Wow, Greg! Yer famous." He was pointing at a picture of an oversized drowned rat, which seemed to resemble me. "I like that headline, "BAND SAVES DAM."

Just then we heard the rumble of a freight train. As I jumped up spilling my coffee, Cranky exclaimed, "Whoa, what's up, Greg!?"

"Didn't you hear that?" I croaked.

"That's just the Burlington Northern 9:20," replied Tom. "Why so jittery?"

Cranky said, "The way you jumped up I would have thought you just won the Lotto!"

"I wish I could win that Lotto," said Tom. "Did you hear it's up to 85 million?"

At that moment I wanted to go back to bed.

GOOSE CALL

If you were walking in the tall grass in northern India with sweat beading on your forehead, and out of ammunition, there is only one sound more terrifying than the roar of a wounded tiger.

Jessica Smith sat on a chair in her bedroom putting the pieces of her clarinet together in anticipation of playing the instrument for only the second time. Jessica's father, in anticipation of her practice session, was out golfing. Her mother was doing a little grocery shopping. Her brother and sister were both at friends' houses and the cat was hiding behind the dryer in the laundry room. Once Jessica had all the pieces put together she applied the size 2 reed and began making sounds. Again, birds began landing in the back yard. By the time she had finished 20 minutes worth of practice there had to have been close to 35 birds out there. She finished practicing and looked out her window. Just like yesterday those large grayish birds with the long black necks were either sifting through the grass or staring at her with a look of anticipation... that is, if they could actually create a look of anticipation.

"You'll be there tomorrow, won't you Greg?" asked Tom Brandston.

"Let me get this straight," I replied, "you want me to get up at 3:30 in the morning, drive out to your farm, trudge a quarter of mile, chop down weeds, and sit in the cold for up to an hour, waiting for your call.....and NOT get paid?"

"Come on, Greg." Tom laughed, "Goose hunting is GREAT!"

"I'm not sure that getting a goose is worth all of that!" I retorted.

"Tell you what," he went on, "afterwards, I'll fix breakfast and we can watch the game. Or you can just stay home with your mother-in-law for the day." Tom knew that Darla's mother was in town for the week.

The thought of spending another day with Darla's mother...... "I'll pick up Cranky on the way," I stated sedately. John Cranklemeyer was a friend of both Tom and me and was almost as avid a hunter as Tom. "But there is one problem you haven't solved since last year."

"And what would that be?" inquired Tom.

"Last year your goose call was awful. Every time you used it the geese flew higher and faster to get away from the noise!"

"If you remember," retorted Tom, "I let both you and Cranky try it. Your attempt sounded like a wounded coyote and Cranky's call brought that elk a'runnin', which trampled our blind, chased us a quarter of a mile and took out the right rear brake light of my pickup."

"I just wish we could actually have something to shoot at this time," I complained.

"It'll be good this year." Tom promised. "I've been practicing my call."

The next morning I woke up to find something akin to Sasquatch staring at me less than three feet away. As I turned away from the bathroom mirror I thought, "What are you doing up at 3:30 AM?" Sasquatch didn't answer.

"Well! Answer me!"

"Wha…"

It was Darla. "What are you doing up at this hour?"

I responded, "Goose huntin'."

After a moment of silence, I either heard the neighbor's dog barking or Darla laughing. The two were indistinguishable. As the barking sounds headed back to the bedroom I went downstairs, had a cup of coffee and some cereal, and then took off to go get Cranky.

As we headed out of town, Cranky stared at a house on his right and said, "Did you notice all the geese in the Smith's backyard yesterday?"

"I didn't go by it yesterday," I responded. "How many were there?"

Cranky replied, "There had to have been at least 30 birds back there. I wonder if they are feeding them."

When we got to Tom's farm, the three of us piled into his pickup and headed out to a remote section of land where he had built a special duck-goose blind. It was so inaccessible that we had to walk part of the way in. When we arrived, I noticed that Tom already had his goose decoys out in the field.

"Do you guys want to hear my goose call?" asked Tom, smiling. "I've been practicing."

"I don't think you should do it this early, Tom," Cranky snickered, "the decoys might fly away, har-de-har!"

Ignoring Cranky with a frown, Tom let loose with something resembling a cross between Tom's pickup horn, a fire engine, and Darla's laugh.

"If you played that at my school, everybody would be under their desks!" I cackled.

Unfortunately, geese don't have desks otherwise they might have stayed under them when they heard Tom's call. Instead, upon hearing Tom's clamor they challenged each other to see who was fastest to get to the next state on their way south. Tom must have thought his call said, "We are your friends. Come down and join us!" However, I think the geese heard, "This is flight control. We advise you to climb to 3,000 feet and continue on your present heading at Mach 2."

And like the last two times we came out here, we spent another miserable day of sitting on the cold, hard ground after little sleep, watching thousands of geese flying high in the sky on a southern heading. We rambled back to Tom's pickup.

"We might have had a chance if you guys would have let me try the call," grumbled Cranky.

"If we were elk hunting, I would agree with you," I countered.

Fortunately, Tom cooked a good breakfast, which meant nothing crawled off the plate while you were eating. After watching UW and WSU pound each other on the football field, Cranky and I headed home. As we came along side the Smiths, I had to pull to a stop. There, in the backyard were fifty of the largest Canadian geese I had ever seen.

"Cranky, we've got to find out how they are getting those geese into their backyard!" I declared.

As we walked up to the front door, Mr. Smith pulled up and began taking his golf clubs out of the trunk. "Hey guys!" he said, "I heard you guys went goose hunting. How'd ya do?"

Feeling too depressed to talk about it I asked, "Have you seen all those geese in your backyard?"

"Yeah, isn't it awful?" said Mr. Smith. Cranky and I just looked at each other. He continued, "The geese leave such a mess we can't even go back there anymore. It all started when Jessica began playing clarinet in your band class, Mr. Olson." Cranky and I looked at each other again.

"Has she been practicing today, Mr. Smith?" I asked.

"Yep! That's why I've been playing a little more golf lately, if you get my drift," he said, with a big grin and a wink. "It seems that the geese are back there every time she is done practicing."

After a moment I said, "Mr. Smith, how would you like to go hunting with us next Saturday?"

"I'd love to!" he said. "Gosh, thanks for the invitation!"

"Oh, by the way," I said, casually, "has Jessica ever come with you on a hunting trip? She might enjoy that."

"That's a great idea," said Mr. Smith.

The next Saturday, Cranky and I knocked on the door of the Smith house. When the door opened there was Mr. Smith and Jessica all bundled up. "I think Jessica should bring her clarinet with her," I blurted.

"Her clarinet?" asked Mr. Smith, with a quizzical look on his face.

"Sure," I said. "After hunting, Tom will make us a good breakfast and I can help Jessica with her clarinet while he is cooking!"

"That is certainly gracious of you," replied Mr. Smith. "Are you sure?"

"I have no doubt!" I responded, with a 'cat who ate the canary' grin across my face.

Sitting in the goose blind I whispered to Jessica, "While you are waiting why don't you play those five notes you learned in beginning band, Jessica."

"Won't I scare away the birds?" asked Jessica.

"They probably won't come for a little while," I countered. "Go ahead."

Mr. Smith was sitting on the other side of Cranky and didn't notice Jessica putting together her instrument. All of a sudden there was a squeal to match anything Tom had ever produced on his goose call.

"Jessica, what are you doing?" yelled her father. However, Jessica's squealing drowned out his question, and she continued. All of a sudden, the sky was filled with geese, many of them trying to land.

There was a volley of gunshot blasts filling the cold morning air. Just as suddenly there was another but different squealing sound coming from the other side of the field.

Tom pointed at the far end of the field and shouted, "Look!"

There, coming at a full run were four very large elk. We grabbed our stuff and took off running. We barely made it to Tom's pickup. Tom, Mr. Smith, and Jessica scrambled into the cab, while Cranky and I jumped into the pickup bed, just as one of the elk smashed into Tom's remaining brake light. Throwing mud into the air, Tom's pickup truck fishtailed all the way back to the road.

"Please pass the gravy, Cranky," asked my wife.

"Sure thing, Darla, he responded. Turning to me he asked, "How's your all-star clarinet player?"

"She is getting an A+ in band!" I announced, smiling.

"Well, she certainly has earned it with all of her EXTRA practice," he remarked, winking at me.

"My only fear is that she will get too good and not be able to use her special talent, if you get my drift," I said, winking back.

"Yeah, but there is always next year's beginning band," he replied, as he helped himself to more mashed potatoes.

"You're probably right," I agreed. And holding my plate up I asked Darla, "May I have seconds on the goose?"

THE GUEST CONDUCTOR

Mabel's Café is an icon in our county. In the last half-century there have been more breakfasts served in this Lost Hollow restaurant than any other restaurant in the region. There may have been almost as many cases of gastronomical distress as well. But most of the locals know what to order and what not to order. Of course, the safest thing to eat at Mabel's has always been breakfast. That's because Mabel doesn't try to do anything too fancy at breakfast. It's the "fancy" dishes that Mabel invents that can put a "cramp" in your plans. Literally.

Being an "insider" of the Mabel's crowd, my two friends and I will find ourselves down here most Saturday mornings, having a late breakfast to start our day. On this particular Saturday, I was sitting next to Tom Brandston, an old school chum and now local farmer just outside of Lost Hollow. Tom was sitting next to my close friend, John "Cranky" Cranklemeyer.

"As I was sayin'," continued Cranky, "ever since that music festival where your band did great, you've become a kinda celebrity around these parts."

"And as I was sayin'," I responded, "There was more than the music that came into play there."

"I know. You blamed that little clarinet player in your band," Cranky replied. "What was his name? Ragweed?"

Tom asked, "What kinda a name is that? Ragweed?"

"It's a long story," I answered. "You'll just have read my memoirs about the Field Trip."

"Memwars? What the heck are memwars? That sounds like one o' Mabel's French concoctions," continued Tom.

"You remember the last time Mabel tried to make a French dish?" queried Cranky. We all laughed and shuddered at the same time.

"That was almost as scary as when Mrs. Stubbleberg sent me and the band on that first ever field trip," I quipped. Laughing, I mentioned, "Do you remember that day when Stubbleberg came in here to Mabel's? I thought I was hearing the soundtrack from that scary Alfred Hitchcock movie. It turned out to be Lyle's bad truck brakes." We all chuckled. Well, actually, Tom guffawed. He didn't know how to chuckle.

I don't know if it was karma, fate, e.s.p., or dumb luck, but just then the door to Mabel's Café swung wide. Through the opening slid the most hideous pair of brown shoes I had seen since I last saw Mrs. Stubbleberg. And wouldn't you know it, hovering right above those shoes was the infamous celebrity herself. She stopped just inside the door and started sweeping the room with those radar eyes of hers, coming to rest on three targets sitting in the corner booth. Tom, Cranky and I always sat in the corner booth.

Mrs. Stubbleberg, the principal of Lost Hollow High School, walked over to our table and fired, "Hello, boys."

"Good morning, Mrs. Stubbleberg," deflected the automatic unison from three grown men who were cowering as if they were just sent to the principal's office. I was impressed. When we were in high school choir we were never able to sing anything in unison.

Many years ago Mrs. Stubbleberg was our 4th grade teacher and her overwhelming aura years later could still make three adult men expect detention.

"How is your breakfast, John," she crooned, fixing a smile on Cranky. I noticed Cranky sitting across from me with a look of innocence that produced an instant golden halo floating just two inches above his scalp. "Teacher's pet!" I thought, remembering that I had that same opinion of him twenty years earlier.

"My breakfast is just wonderful, Mrs. Stubbleberg," Cranky replied, and then continued with a sugary, "Could I order you some?" And, "My, you look lovely today." I was hoping she would order pancakes because she certainly wouldn't need syrup.

"No, no," she intoned, smiling that shark smile of hers. She turned to look directly at me. I immediately felt like a harbor seal that had strayed too far from shore.

"I actually came here to find Greg and be the first to congratulate him."

"Congratulate Greg?" asked Tom.

"Oh, yes," continued Mrs. S., who looked like she was contemplating playing with her seal a little before satisfying her hunger. "It seems the high marks received by the Lost Hollow High School Band has drawn some attention this way."

"Really?" queried Cranky, as he turned his smile towards me. However, I hadn't taken my eyes off the shark...I mean... Mrs. Stubbleberg. I had a slight foreboding in seeing how she licked her lips. I was wondering if this harbor seal should be diving under the table.

"The Seattle Symphony is looking to do an outreach up north," she continued. "They are going to have their most recent composer-in-residence direct one of our regional bands at the Seattle Symphony Hall to encourage music education in our state. So they looked at last spring's regional festival and chose a band who had some of the highest marks: Lost Hollow High School Band!"

Just before I fainted I heard the theme music from that Hitchcock movie. The next thing I remember was waking up, shivering.

"Wha, wha, what happened?" I asked.

"You passed out," Tom replied. "We were going to pour a pitcher of water on you but Mabel thought ice would be less messy." I looked down to see that I was the middle part of an ice sandwich. I shivered and tried to brush off all that ice.

"The excitement must have overwhelmed you!" cried Cranky. "I don't blame you. That IS really awesome!"

"You don't understand," I sighed. "Our high marks at the music festival weren't entirely because of our musicianship. There was..."

Cranky punched me in the arm. "There you go being Mr. Humble again!" he exclaimed, laughing. "What a great opportunity for your kids!" he continued.

"Yeah, Greg," persisted Tom. "How many bands ever get a chance like that!

"I guess you're right," I agreed, hoping this composer-in-residence did not have high expectaions. Grinning, I continued, "I guess I overreacted. I even heard Lyle's bad truck brakes again." Laughing, I said, "I sure wish Lyle would get his brakes fixed!"

"Lyle hasn't been in town for weeks, Greg," replied Tom. "He's down in Oregon doing some hauling for a lumber company and won't be back 'till next month."

I just stared at my two friends.

During the next month, our band really started getting down to work. There were even some kids who practiced outside of class time, although I tried to make them understand that playing tuba or snare drum in their math class might not endear them to their teacher.

One day, as I was locking up the band room at the end of a long day, I ran into the custodian, Sven. He had white hair, a white beard and was wearing his customary denim overalls and an oil stained baseball cap. I noticed he was carrying a bucket of white powder.

"Whadya got in the bucket, Sven?"

"Oh, hi, Greg. Dis stuff iss to remoof dat ant problem we haff outside da auditorium. Since ants haff been coming into it, I'm goink to sprinkle some uf dis stuff around da base uf da buildink. Since no one will be yoosink it for a couple uf weeks, dis iss a gude time ta do dat."

"Well, good luck, Sven. Say, maybe you could sprinkle some of that around the band room to get rid of the wrong notes problem we have."

"A-hut, a-hut, a-hut," chuckled Sven as he walked down the hallway. "Yer such a kidder, Greg. Dere's nutting made in ta worlt wut is dat strong! A-hut, a-hut, a-hut, a-hut." As I stared at Sven's back, I had a foreboding of the guest conductor event soon to take place. Maybe this was a good time to come down with the flu, measles, and chicken pox. I wondered how sick I could sound on the phone. Better yet, I could have Billy call for me. That kid was a pro. If I could only get him to practice his drum as much as he practiced the call-in-sick voice….

I was relieved to find out that the Seattle Symphony folks just expected us to play our usual material and have their composer-in-residence, Vladimer Feinkov, direct it. Thinking that Feinkov might have a different idea about what "usual material" might be, I decided it might be time to move on from Mary Had A Little Lamb. We started working on a much more complex piece.

"Mr. Olson," asked one of the trumpet players Jimmy Thornbush, "why do we have learn a song about a bridge that falls down in England? I liked the Lamb song, even though everyone knows that Priscilla's family is the one that owns the sheep around these parts and not Mary." Jimmy smiled and winked at Priscilla, who was our blushing principal flute player.

"Jimmy," I countered, "two months on one song is enough. It's time for you to learn new material." Smiling, I continued, "That's how you get better!"

In spite of the grumbling and the innuendos about the band teacher being a taskmaster, we got to work and within a month felt ready for the guest conductor. When the day arrived, along with the Seattle Symphony composer, I was called down to the main office to meet our esteemed maestro. As I walked into Mrs. Stubbleberg's office, I could see a very tall thin man, dressed in a full tuxedo with shoes that actually shined, conversing with our principal.

"Greg," began Mrs. Stubbleberg, "this is Dr. Feinkov from the Seattle Symphony."

"Oh, please. Call me Vladimer," the tall man interrupted, reaching out his hand.

As I took his hand I said, "The kids are looking forward to meeting you, Valad..er Vela..uh..Dr. Feinkov." I was hoping I was being truthful. "They've been practicing on some new material for the concert."

"Oh, they don't have to do that," he replied, waving his jeweled hand. "I have composed a new work for this occasion. It is a march in the style of John Philip Sousa."

"But, but..." I exclaim.

"That's wonderful!" interjected Mrs. Stubbleberg. "You mean we will be having a premier of a new work right here in Lost Hollow?"

"But, but..."

"That is correct, Mrs. Stubbleberg," Feinkov continued, "and I have invited the Seattle Tribune, Seattle Journal, and two television stations to come and critique the performance."

As the room went dark I remember thinking, "Lyle's brakes... Lyle's brakes..."

As I came to, there was Mrs. S. & Cranky leaning over me. "Greg, you've got to get more sleep," Cranky said, while fanning me with a file folder. I could read the consternation on his face.

"I see you have consternation," I mentioned, grinning on one side of my mouth.

"Oh, I haven't had 'consternation' since the last time I ate lunch at Mabel's. The fiber pills have really helped!"

"Where is Dr. Feinkov?" I queried.

Mrs. S. replied, "I had the custodian take him down to meet your band kids."

"What!?" I yelled, as I jumped up and raced out of the office.

"It's ok, Greg!" Cranky shouted back. "Even though the custodian avoids the band room, he still knows how to find it!"

As I opened the band room door, panting, my fears proved to be founded. Dr. Feinkov was nowhere to be seen. Over the cacophony of sounds I yelled, "Where is the conductor!" Eventually the sounds dwindled down to a dull roar.

Ragweed asked, "What did you say, Mr. Olson?"

"Where is our Guest Conductor?"

"Dr. Feinkov is over there in your office, Mr. Olson," said one of the drummers, Billy Middleton, as he pointed with a drumstick at the door to my right. I quickly went to my office but could not see Feinkov anywhere. I started to head back out to the main room when I saw a shoe sticking out from underneath my desk.

As I bent over to look I asked, "Dr. Feinkov, is that you?" But he didn't hear me because his hands were over his ears. So I tapped his knee, causing him to shoot straight up about two feet. That might not have been such a bad thing except for my desk being in the way. The cacophony of sounds that erupted from my office caused the cacophony of sounds in the band room to completely stop. I quickly checked underneath the desk to see if he had broken anything but was satisfied that the desk was entirely fine. Feinkov, on the other hand, had a golf-ball-sized welt on top of his head. I won't bore you with the details, but I finally got him out of my office and standing in front of the kids.

"Students," I began, "this is Dr. Feinkov, the guest conductor I was telling you about."

Billy blurted out, "He's a doctor, too?"

"He's probably here to heal all your bad notes!" Jimmy yelled back at Billy, joining the laughter from the class until his mouth became stuffed with a bass drum mallet.

"Billy, please remove the mallet from Jimmy's mouth. I can't afford to keep replacing those."

Priscilla intoned, "Shall we play our new song we have been working on for Dr. Feinkov?"

"Well," answered Feinkov, eyeing Billy apprehensively, "I have actually composed a new song that I am going to teach you." At that statement, the entire band class dropped their jaws and started eyeing Feinkov apprehensively.

One of the clarinets asked, "Is it as hard as London Bridge Is Falling Down?"

This elicited a roar of laughter from Feinkov while the kids were looking at one another to see if anyone other than Feinkov got the joke. When Feinkov turned to look at me, I joined in with nervous laughter. The students, catching the cue, joined in with some forced laughter as well, even though it was obvious none of them had a clue about anything humorous.

I helped Feinkov hand out parts. Ragweed blurted out, "I think you gave me a flute part Dr. Feinkov. These notes are too high."

"Nonsense," indicated Feinkov as he scanned Ragweed's part. "This is in the perfect range for the low 3rd clarinet. Now who is going to play the higher 1st clarinet part?" Ragweed's jaw fell onto his music stand.

Billy, the percussionist, held up his music facing me and stated, "Mr. Olson, I think someone must have spilt ink on my music. It's covered with a lot of black stuff."

"Those are called notes, Billy."

Various other comments wafted out of the mouths of my adorable students, but eventually we got all the parts handed out and were ready for Feinkov to conduct.

Smiling, Feinkov tapped his music stand with his baton and announced, "OK, children. Let's give this a go!"

As he was ready to give the downbeat a hand shot up. Our tuba player, Blap (also known as Tommy), asked, "Dr. Feinkov, how do you play the first note?"

I suppose the look of shock on Feinkov's face was due to the fact that the note Blap was referring to was the first note that a tuba player learns in beginning band. With his mouth wide open, Feinkov turned to me to say something. He moved his jaw but nothing came out. But I quickly solved Blap's problem the same way I solve all of the fingering problems in band class.

"Look at the fingering chart in the back of your band book, Blap."

"Thanks, Mr. Olson. Gee, you're such a great teacher!" I smiled at Blap and turned to see that Feinkov's jaw had stopped moving. It was in the position of wide open. I looked over his shoulder at the conductor part for this new composition and surmised that getting this band to try to play THAT would be like trying to cut down a cedar tree with a pocketknife. So I did the only conscientious thing a person in my position could do.

"Dr. Feinkov," I announced, "while you are teaching the students your new song, I'll just go check to make sure the auditorium will be all set up." I took his jaw-moving-with-no-sound-coming-out as a signal that he agreed and quickly bolted from the room. When I got to the auditorium I found Sven, holding his cap in his hands and scratching his head.

"You're looking a little perplexed, Sven. What's up?"

"Vell, I don't get it. It usually takes a veek or tooo fer deese ants ta go away. But deese ants ver gone da day after I sprinkled da powder. I vunder iff dey moved somevere else?"

"Maybe that stuff was powerful enough to just exterminate them, Sven."

"Maybe," replied Sven, still scratching his head.

I went in and saw that all the risers and chairs were in place for the big event tomorrow night. So I headed back to the band room. I was astonished to hear some semblance of organized sound coming out of the band room. The band had just finished Feinkov's song as I entered the room. The smiling face of Feinkov was quite different from the face of shock I had left earlier. Ragweed blurted out, "We sound pretty good, don't we Mr. Olson?"

"I would say so," I responded.

My puzzled look must have been why Feinkov volunteered, "I came up with a system where each section knows when to play their parts." He turned back to the band.

"Now remember, students, I will give each section a cue. Flutes, whenever I point at you with my left hand, I want you to play that scale. Trumpets, my right hand means I want you to play those accented triplets. When I stab the air with my baton, clarinets, start playing that trill." To Calvin Smith he said, "When I stamp the podium, play the bass drum to my beat. And snare drummer play the off-beats in between the bass drum hits. Do you all have that?"

Statements of confirmation and nods of heads were the responses by the band. Just then the bell rang and the kids headed to their next class.

"Well, Mr. Olson, this band is at a different level than I expected," offered Feinkov, as he peered at me over his bifocals. The one-eyebrow-raised on the left side of his face had me believing that this might not be exactly a full-fledged compliment. Rather than continue that line of conversation I responded, "Do you think you will be able to remember all those cues you are giving the kids? That seems to be lot to think about while you are directing!"

As Feinkov straightened up his 6'2" frame, he raised his head so that he could peer right down his nose at me. "You forget who I am, Mr. Olson! The great Dr. Feinkov can do that and much more!" The last statement was punctuated with a stab of his baton into the ceiling. Literally. I left Feinkov to work his baton out of the ceiling tile and headed home for a good night's sleep. The Thursday night concert was tomorrow and I knew I'd need my rest.

The next day proved uneventful. We just had the usual elk running through the elementary school's playground, 6 year old Samuel Perry playing with a cat that had stripes and having to be sent home for a week until the smell died away, and Charlie Queznell bringing a cutthroat trout into his 5th grade class for show & tell. The fact that the fish was two days old just added to the interest of the display.

As far as how the band rehearsal went for that night's performance: it was uneventful. That's because I wasn't about to try to recreate Feinkov's acrobatic cueing technique. Instead, we just watched an appropriate movie to prepare the kids emotionally.

"Wow, Mr. Olson," whispered Ragweed, "that guy has a great casting technique!"

Priscilla interjected with a scowl, "Mr. Olson, why are we watching a fly-fishing movie on the day of our concert?!"

"Shhhh," came the response from all the boys in the room.

I whispered back, "Priscilla, one day a student from this class might decide to be a band teacher. The technique that this fisherman displays with his fishing rod could be used with a director's baton. Now I need you to be quiet so that we can concentrate. Did you notice that side-arm style of his?"

Priscilla slumped back in her chair with her arms folded, an ugly looking frown, and a dark cloud hovering right over her blonde head.

At the end of the school day kids came and got their instruments and I reminded them to be early for that night's concert. "Don't forget to watch for Dr. Feinkov's cues!" I shouted to the departing students.

That evening, I showed up early to make sure everything was in place. I found Sven all dressed up near the stage door. "Wow, Sven! I see you are wearing your coveralls instead of your overalls. This must be a special event for you!"

"Vell, I hurd dat all dose TV and noospaper people ver goink ta be here und I vanted ta look guud fer dem." The thought of all the media folk coming to town almost brought my asthma back.

"Did you ever discover where those ants went?" I queried.

"Nope. I dink dey haf all gone ta ant heaven."

I left Sven and headed around to the front of the building to steer the band students towards the warm-up room. Doing so, I ran right into one of the local Seattle TV crews. Mrs. Stubbleberg was talking with a man holding a microphone. She had a saintly-looking smile on her face. I didn't know she could do that. Hoping not to be noticed, I abruptly turned to head back to the stage door.

"Greg!" I stopped, afraid to turn around.

"Greg, I have some people I would like you to meet," announced Mrs. Stubbleberg. I turned to face the inevitable. Trying to smile, I was sure my grin resembled more of a grimace.

"Mr. Olson?" A reporter shoved a microphone in my face as the camera guy zoomed in on my grimace. "Mr. Olson, are you excited to have your students directed by the great Dr. Feinkov?"

As I stared at the camera, I realized that thousands of people would be watching this news clip. Awestruck, I promptly froze into a lop-sided grin and totally forget everything I knew…my name, why I was there, my occupation….

"Come on, Mr. Olson, being the band director of Lost Hollow High School you must have some opinion of tonight's event!"

"Band director! Yes, I'm the band director!" It felt good to find reality again. "Well," I began, giving the camera my most serious and studious expression, "Dr. Feinkov is able to get sounds out of those kids that I've never been able to produce." How true that statement was.

Just then, a bunch of band kids showed up and I began directing them where to go. Once all the kids were collected in the warm-up room, I reminded them, "Now don't forget your cues, kids. Do you all remember what Dr. Feinkov's motions mean?" With nods of assent coming from the students, I started heading for the auditorium and said, "OK. Five minutes to go. Everyone get into your concert seats."

I headed out to the auditorium and found Darla, my wife, sitting next to an empty seat in the middle of the seventh row. On the other side of the seat were Cranky and Tom. As I sat down, I saw Mrs. Stubbleberg leaving stage right to grab a microphone in front center stage.

"Good evening, people of Lost Hollow and guests!" With that last word she turned to smile at the reporters and camera people. "We have a special honor tonight to have Seattle Symphony's own Dr. Feinkov here to direct the Lost Hollow Band!" She waved her arm behind her to the 38 uniformed students sitting behind the music stands. A big cheer went up from the audience, which caused all the students to smile. I thought, "This is going to be an awesome night!"

"And now, please welcome the esteemed Dr. Feinkov!"

From stage right strode the lanky form of the tall Feinkov in his customary tuxedo, but with very long tails. He bowed to the applauding audience and then stepped onto the podium. Placing his bifocals on his nose, he raised his baton and began the downbeat. I have to say that I was watching artistry in conducting, as he was able to give multiple cues at once, stabbing the air, gyrating his torso, pointing a finger, tapping a foot, and more. Unbelievably, the resulting sounds were real band sounds. To include the bass drummer he started pounding his foot, whereupon the bass drummer caught the cue and began playing in time.

There have been many hypothesis about what caused the next event, but I personally think it was the foot pounding. All of a sudden, Feinkov jumped up and when he landed back down, he started an erratic stomping of both his feet, causing Calvin, the bass drummer, to start a wild banging on his instrument. Feinkov's arms went wild, thereby creating a most unorthodox cueing system. This in turn generated the most amazing conflict of sounds that Lost Hollow had ever heard, sounds that were even MORE original than the sounds created by the beginning band. As Feinkov was unpredictably leaping, stomping and stabbing the air with his baton I noticed that even the notes on his music sheets were moving.

I turned to my friend. "Cranky!" Pointing, I yelled over the tumult. "Do you see that?"

"Yeah!" He called back, grinning. "I didn't know your flutes could play and dance at the same time!"

I turned to see the first row of the band standing up and doing some kind of Irish jig, with rhythms not entirely unlike Feinkov's. I was quite proud of their ability to maintain their cacophony of sounds at the same time. But as I peered at Feinkov's moving notes, I noticed they were not only moving around the page, but also crawling down his music stand. Following the trail down, I saw that they mostly covered his podium and were crawling around the floor near the musicians.

Feinkov's movements were later credited with the creation of the new dance in our county called "the Conductor."

But eventually, Feinkov finally leapt off the podium, landing with a thud onto the stage floor. This evidently was the cue for a last loud note, along with a bass drum hit and cymbal crash. For two seconds there was absolute silence. And then the media people started cheering and applauding as they jumped out of their seats. Not wanting to seem like hicks from the sticks, the rest of the audience followed suit and gave a loud, rousing standing ovation. Feinkov stared at the audience with a look of amazement on his face while the band was all smiles. Billy was pumping his fist in the air and Blap clapped Ragweed on the shoulder, which almost flattened the little clarinet player, who was still dancing the gigue.

Feinkov stomped off to the side of the stage, but the applause would not diminish until he came out to the stage to acknowledge the ovation. As he came back out to the middle of the stage the clapping elevated in volume while many shouts of "bravo" and "encore" were hurled from the audience. Feinkov simply looked dumbfounded. But he did have the presence to have the band stand up, which caused another wave of cheering. The kids were soaking it in; all except the first row of musicians, who were dancing to some inner music while all the little black notes were running all over the floor around their feet.

Of course, by now you have realized that those "notes" were really ants. It seems Sven's extermination technique was the cause of a whole colony of ants to hide underneath the auditorium. It only took Feinkov's pounding to aggravate the little critters; especially since their nest was directly under Feinkov's podium.

These were obviously cultural ants, because the whole colony of them came up from the floorboards to enjoy the music. Being the cultural ants they were, they decided that it is improper to sit on the stage during a performance so they headed over the edge of the stage to find a seat in the audience. Once the audience realized that ants were infesting them, they graciously gave up their seats to the little creatures and vacated the auditorium in less than two minutes. Sven was so please at the speed in which the auditorium was emptied that he figured he would ask permission to use the same audience-clearing technique for future concerts so that he can get in there to sweep up.

That Saturday I walked into Mabel's and saw my two cronies sitting at the corner table. As I slid into the booth, Tom was holding up the Seattle Journal to page three. In large, bold print letters at the very top was written, "MUSICAL ARTISTRY IS IN LOST HOLLOW!" For a moment I sat there with a stunned look on my face. Then I snatched the paper out of Tom's hands and began to read the article.

"There was Musical Magic on Thursday night as the great Dr. Feinkov directed his latest creation. However, it was not the Seattle Symphony performing his work but the Lost Hollow High School Band. They did an exemplary job of matching every cue, inflection, gyration, swirl and stab of Feinkov's baton! Watching Feinkov was like watching a ballet. One moment he was the epitome of grace; the next, he was the inventor of some new dance full of twists and turns that one would think not humanly possible.

His composition was the wildest freshest new work this paper has critiqued in a decade. Our compliments also go to the Lost Hollow Band and their director, Greg Olson. If you ever get a chance to hear this piece, you MUST go listen. The title of the piece is ...."

"Whoa!" exclaimed Cranky. "Did you hear that, Tom? We are sitting in the company of the rich and famous!"

Tom smiled at me and responded, "How 'bout just 'famous'."

Cranky announced, "Well, I'm buyin' yer breakfast, Greg, just to show appreciation for our celebrity!" I had no doubt that he overheard me ordering just toast. Maybe it wasn't too late to get Mabel to change my order.

Tom said, "Cranky, you interrupted Greg's readin'. I wanna to hear the rest." Tom pointed at the paper in my hand and offered, "Go on, Greg."

"Well, there's just one more sentence," I replied as I glanced back down at the Journal. Then I looked back up to my two expectant friends with a look of awe on my face.

"Well!" they both exclaimed in harmony.

I continued, "The title of the piece is The March Of The Fire Ants." At that moment you could have seen two frozen men with coffee cups about an inch from their lips.

STATE CONVENTION

Over the years I have struggled over obstacles, failures, misfortunes, setbacks, adjusting to change and the need to practice. I have dealt with stubbornness, ridicule, lack of support, discouragements, and stumbling blocks. There have been mistakes made along the way, wasted energy, and downright failures.

But enough about fishing. Today, I would like to focus your attention on a special situation that came up for our high school band. We were invited to perform for the State Music Convention. Yes, really. Somehow, probably due to some mix-up, the Lost Hollow High School Band received the invitation.

It was not really that big of a deal. We would only be performing for a couple thousand of some of the finest music instructors in the state, not to mention many administrators, which would include my principal and our school superintendent. Not feeling any pressure, I made the following casual comment to my 8th grade band class, "Kids, starting today, I want you all to practice three hours per day, come in for extra rehearsals four nights per week, and drop out of all your other subjects!"

I know that they could tell the seriousness of my demeanor by the way they only laughed for 30 seconds instead of the typical non-stop cackles. The strange part was that half the class was willing to honor my request, especially Billy, who was flunking Language Arts and PE.

You are probably wondering how my group could possibly be invited to perform at such a prestigious event. It seems some organizers of the convention had read an article by a Seattle paper commenting how our band created completely new sounds at a local concert. This was during an event in which a guest conductor from the Seattle Symphony came to Lost Hollow. But that's a different story altogether.

At any rate, that invitation was also sent to my principal. She met with me to see if I would accept the honor. The conversation went something like this:

"Greg, you ARE going to accept!"

"But, but but…"

And that was about the extent of the conversation, even though I left off a few "but's."

This convention was put on to demonstrate new practices and techniques, and to help new teachers in music education. I had actually attended this convention in the last couple of years to see what it was about and to better educate myself in new techniques of teaching band. Part of the reason I went was that my college degree was actually History and I probably could use a little help in the music area. Another reason is that the convention was held next to one of the best salmon producing rivers in the state. However, I DID pick up a couple of tidbits like: rehearsal technique, classroom discipline, motivational skills, how to read conductor scores, names of notes, how to play band instruments, and about a thousand other things. I imagine going back to college to get a music degree might have helped, too.

Whenever I attended this convention, performance groups from various schools gave concerts for the music educators. These are some of the top groups in the state. However, I found them a bit lacking. Sure, they could play all the notes and rhythms perfectly and sound practically professional. But none of them had the kind of special techniques that MY students possess.

For example, I never heard a single percussionist from another school hit the bass drum as hard as Billy Middleton, who is one of my drummers. Billy has a two-hand technique that could have rivaled Babe Ruth. You might have just noticed that I called Billy a drummer. That's because there is a distinct difference between Drummer and Percussionist. But that difference is discussed in depth in another story I have penned.

Also, these outstanding bands from our Washington State have overall boring sounds. None of them create something new and daring, such as the sounds created by Barney Wertelmeyer (a.k.a Ragweed) on his clarinet. I can pretty much conclude that there is no one in the world who can produce sounds like Barney can while holding that weapon in his hands. And when the tuba players from those other bands play, I never feel the floor shake, like when my own student, Blap, lets loose.

However, not wanting to shake the confidence of those bands and directors, I will always applaud their performances. It is very nice to see that hundreds of my colleagues feel the same way. I just don't think they need to STAND and applaud like they do, even though I know they are doing that because they are tired of sitting and being bored.

I remember one particular performance in which a band was playing a piece that my own high school band was working on. They not only played all the right notes, but played with excitement and character, and twice as fast as my band can play it. When the audience stood up and applauded at the end I began thinking maybe they weren't standing due to boredom. The fact that this group was only in fourth grade probably didn't help my ego much either.

So now I had to bring MY band to this event and I was a bit apprehensive. I actually started trying to READ the music and even required my band to practice. The cacophony of sounds heard in the evenings those days in Lost Hollow would make you cringe. Maybe that was because all the dogs decided to join in with my practicing students, not to mention the wailing parents.

"I'm telling you, Tom, I'm nervous about it being out of tune, not being able to keep time, and all of the ragged sounds," I said, forlornly.

"I think yer gonna have to take it in this time, Greg," he replied, while looking under the hood of my Ford. "Hey, speakin' of outta tune, how's yer band comin' along? Guffaw, guffaw, guffaw. You gonna be ready for that convention of yers? Guffaw." When Tom laughed he sounded like a cross between a mule and a barking dog.

"The car sounds better than my band, Tom."

Tom Brandston, the farmer, has been a good friend for many years. The fact that he has a great duck and goose hunting setup and one of the best stocked fishing ponds on his property hasn't hurt much, either.

"Just give 'em time, tighten up here, loosen up there, and they'll be ready to go in time," he said. "By the way, when IS your performance?"

"In a couple o' months, Tom, but I don't think you can tune the band like a car!"

"I dunno. Accordin' to what you told me, teachin' those band insterments is quite a bit like runnin' a car. When they goes flat you give 'em more air, when the rhythm isn't right you take it apart to see what needs fixin', make 'em go faster or slower, sometimes push 'em, tune 'em, fix 'em, and you steer 'em with your hands."

"Possibly, Tom," I retorted, "but I think THIS driver is running out of gas."

Tom was right. After the next couple of months were over, the band somehow was beginning to produce tones that sounded a bit more human in nature versus the usual wild African animal ones.

"Do we get to take a charter bus, Mr. Olson?" The question came during the last rehearsal.

"No, Harvey. You get to ride on a school bus."

"That's too bad Mr. Olson, because if we were on a charter bus we could see this cool movie I have about a guy with a chain saw, and…"

"I'm sorry, Harvey, but you'll just have to watch THAT movie at home."

"Mr. Olson?" There was a hand raised in the percussion section. "Can we bring CD's? I have a cool rap CD and lyrics are mostly ok, and….."

"If you bring head phones you can bring listening devices, class, but we will NOT be playing YOUR music on the bus system," I countered. "People, we've already gone over everything. Don't forget your IMU!" I said, as the bell rang. We had a way of remembering our gear by the acronym, IMU, which stood for Instrument, Music, and Uniform.

The next morning, I was having breakfast down at Mabel's with Tom Brandston and John "Cranky" Cranklemeyer.

"Ya ready fer today's trip?" mumbled Tom, through a mouthful of hashbrowns.

"I remember that first field trip you took a few years ago," interrupted Cranky, laughing, "where this clarinet player…"

"I'd rather NOT relive that event, if you don't mind, Cranky!" I huffed. "Let's just say I've learned a thing or two since that time."

"Well, one thing's fer sure," said Cranky, with his usual encouragement. "There's a lot more pressure on you this time. I hope you don't bomb!"

Immediately, there was a huge explosion right outside the front door!

Tom said to me, "Would you get out from underneath the table! That was just Lyle's pickup truck backfirin' when he shut it off." I wasn't sure what frayed my nerves more, my band or Lyle's pickup truck.

At school we double and triple checked everybody's IMU and headed out to the bus. As I was standing there I heard, "Well, hello again!"

It was the 110-year-old bus driver from that first field trip! All of a sudden short, high pitch violin notes began coming out of nowhere.

"Mr. Olson," said one of the students. "What are you doing under the bus?"

"Didn't you hear those sounds?" I responded.

"That was Lyle Jefferson's pickup truck going by!"

As we were getting ready to head out of town for the State Music Convention in Ellensburg, I noticed that the bus driver still had those blocks taped to her shoes from that LAST experience.

"I see you still use those blocks, Ms…, Ms…"

"It's Mrs. Steinworter and yup, cain't reach the brake pedal or accelerator without 'em," she interrupted. "Cain't believe the duct tape has lasted this long!" I was sure apprehension was written all over my face.

As I turned to face the back of the bus one of my students said, "What is that written on your face, Mr. Olson? A-p-p-……"

"OK, people. Everybody have a seat so we can go…."

Immediately the bus jerked into motion and we were off, even though the band director was face down in the middle of the aisle.

The bus driver turned to say, "You DID say go didn't you? I'm a little hard of hearing. Hey! Where'd ya go?" As I picked myself up off the floor of the bus she continued, "Oh, there you are." And then with a scowl, "I'm sorry but you'll have to remain seated when the bus is in motion!"

Returning the scowl I countered with, "How long until we get there?"

She responded, "'bout 3 hours if we don't break down."

"Break down!?"

"Yup. This bus tends to break down a third o' the time," she replied while cackling something that was supposed to resemble laughter. "But don't worry, they still pay me even when we're just sittin'."

When we got to the Cascade Mountains the bus really started chugging as it tried to make the climb to Snoqualmie Pass. I was fairly concerned that it wasn't going to make it.

"Sputter!" "Groan!" "Cluck, cluck!" went the sounds.

Squinting, the bus driver turned to me and said, "Makin' those sounds won't make the bus go any faster, Olson! Besides, the bus makes enough sounds by itself without your help!"

With a morbid expression I responded, "We can't be going more than 20 miles an hour. If we don't get a move on, we won't make it in time for the performance!"

"Well, once we get to the pass, we'll make better time goin' down the other side," she replied. "Say, the duct tape on my right foot is startin' to come off. Could you press it back down?"

It took about an hour to get all the way up to Snoqualmie Pass. When we finally started heading down the other side the kids all cheered. I was thankful that our speed started improving. I saw the speedometer had jumped all the way up to 50 mph. A big smile spread across my face when I realized all the traffic wasn't zooming by as if we were standing still. I noticed the big evergreen trees whizzing by, majestic snow covered peaks slowly fading to the rear, and beautiful blue-green lakes on either side to complete the picture. I thought to myself, "Ya know, we have a beautiful state and field trips aren't so bad." Mistaken thoughts.

"Wow, Mrs. Steinworter, I didn't know a bus could go 70 miles-per-hour. Are you sure it's safe?" I asked, with a nervous, "ha, ha."

"Ha, ha," she cackled back. "I'm not really tryin' ta go 70, but that block I had taped to the bottom of my shoe came off and I cain't quite reach the brake pedal." As she squirmed in her seat she grunted, "Yup, cain't quite reach the brake pedal. I'd look fer it but I'm kinda busy." I nervously glanced at the speedometer, which had reached 76 mph.

"It's got to be around here somewhere!" I exclaimed from the floor near the driver's foot pedals. Fortunately, I discovered it under the driver's seat. Suddenly, the bus veered left then right, slamming my head into one of the legs of the driver's seat.

"OW!" I yelled. "Can't you keep this bus steady!"

She responded, "Sorry, I just didn't want to squish that little sports car we went sailin' past."

I got up on my knees holding the wooden block that I found and looked at the speedometer. It read 87 mph.

"If yer eyes get any bigger, Olson, they're goin' to pop right oudda yer head!"

I looked up to see her smiling at me with a half-toothed grin. I turned to look forward and saw that we were barreling down on a big tractor-trailer rig and realized how wrong the bus driver was. My eyes DID get bigger but stayed in my head.

"LOOK OUT!" I screamed.

Mrs. Steinworter saw the truck in the nick-of-time and swerved left, causing me to roll down the steps. I hit the doors hard but unfortunately kept going. The only thing that kept me from rolling all the way out onto the racing asphalt was that my foot caught in the little handrail. There I was, with my body lying on the stairs and my head just outside the bus in the rushing air-stream. The air was blowing so hard against my face I could hardly open my eyes to see the road sign racing right for my head! I opened my mouth to scream but before I could, there was a violent jerk on my arm. I found myself practically standing straight up staring into the grinning face of Blap, who, at 275 pounds, was the biggest person on the bus.

"Mr. Olson," Blap chuckled, "I always get in trouble when I do that kinda'stuff on the bus. I really think you should set a better example for the kids." Chuckle, chuckle.

As Blap made his way back to his seat, my mouth was moving up and down somewhat like a cutthroat trout but no sound was coming out. I didn't have much time to think about what just happened because we were barreling down on two tractor-trailer rigs that were side-by-side, blocking the two-lane highway.

"Where's that block!?" yelled Mrs. Steinworter, who was desperately squirming, trying to reach the brake pedals.

"I'm afraid I lost it out the door when I fell!" I blurted in response, as I stared at the approaching disaster.

Those big, massive trucks seemed like they were going backwards because of the speed in which we were overtaking them. When the backs of those rigs were just yards away, I closed my eyes bracing for the impact. Instantly, I found myself in the aisle again as the bus veered violently to the right. I looked up to see the trucks streaming backwards past the left side of the bus. I quickly turned to the front and saw that were fishtailing on the graveled shoulder of the highway. To the right I saw about a 300 foot drop-off. We hit the guardrail and there were all kinds of screams.

As the bus tilted right onto 2 wheels, the bus driver yelled, "Mr. Olson, stop screaming so I can concentrate!"

As the bus slammed back down onto all four wheels, I could just make out a sign that said, "Ellensburg 2 miles."

I bellowed to the driver, "There's an off-ramp to Ellensburg ahead. If it goes up, maybe it can slow us down!"

"I saw the sign!" screeched Mrs. Steinworter.

Even though the bus was beginning to slow down on the level highway, the ramp still seemed like it was coming up awful fast. As we veered right onto the ramp I watched the speedometer as it showed us slowing: 50, 45, 40, 35, 30. Unfortunately, we were still doing 30 as we barreled through the stop sign with Mrs. Steinworter spinning the wheel to the left. Of course, this caused us to end up on our 2 right wheels again.

The boys in the back of the bus were cheering with shouts of "Cool!" "Awesome!" "Tight!" while the band director was countering with, "Aaargh!" "Yow!" and "Help!" The yelling didn't seem to help us slow down any more rapidly than what was natural so I stopped. I glanced at the speedometer to see it was now below 25 mph and dropping. I looked at my watch. I couldn't believe that we had made it here so fast that we still had ten minutes before we were to perform. I turned around to see the entire busload of students with grins on every one of their faces.

"Wow, Mr. Olson!" exclaimed Ragweed. "This is the best bus ride I have ever been on!" There were immediately all kinds of sounds of agreement and applause from the other smiling riders. Jimmy Thornbush shouted, "Yeah, Mr. Olson, can we do that again!" The dark cloud above my head didn't seem to dampen their spirits any.

"Look, you guys," I responded. "It looks like we just might make it in time to play our concert, so I want you all to get your instruments and music out of your cases so we can just get out and play as soon as we get there, ok?" The kids started getting their gear out. I turned to see the concert hall approaching so I looked at the speedometer: 15 mph.

"How are we going to stop this thing?" I blurted to Mrs. Steinworter.

"I dunno!" was the response. "I cain't see any ramps or hills."

A minute later we could see the concert hall on the right and we were only going 10 miles per when we made the turn onto the side street leading to the hall.

"Hey, look!" Mrs. Steinworter exclaimed. "There's a concrete ramp leadin' to the back stage. That'd probably stop us!"

"Are you sure?"

"Nope."

But before I could officially file a protest, Mrs. Steinworter turned sharply left heading right for the ramp. A couple of men were standing on the ramp and when they saw the bus heading right for them, they started frantically waving their arms as if to say, "You're going the wrong way!"

They must have figured that our bus didn't speak in sign-language because they jumped off the ramp in the knick-of-time. The bus hit the ramp and then slowed…but not to a complete stop! It must have been going only 1 mph as it slowly inched its way onto the stage. It just kind-of pushed the chairs which were in position on the stage out of the way. That was just enough obstruction to cause the bus to stop, dead-center of the stage.

As I looked out the bus's left windows, I saw about three thousand awe-struck faces staring back at me. It now dawned on me that these were the faces of the audience that had come to hear my band perform.

"Quick!" I yelled. "Get up the march. When I say 'go,' everybody open up the windows. Then we'll start playing!"

"Go!"

Two days later down at Mabels, Cranky was holding up the Lost Hollow Gazette as I was digging my fork into a steaming omelet.

"Did ya find the story about the band?" Tom asked before taking a slurp of his coffee.

"Hold yer horses, Tom!" Cranky answered with a scowl. "It says it's on page two." Cranky rustled the paper and then stated, "Ah, here it is!" Cranky began reading:

"This last Tuesday, the music educators at a recent state-wide convention were treated to another of Lost Hollow High School Band's innovative concerts. It seems that the band performed an entire concert from a bus on the stage. We are not sure where director Greg Olson gets his inventive ideas, but it seems that this one was a huge success at the convention. When asked what caused him to choose this medium, Mr. Olson stated, "We were trying to portray 'Life On The Road'."

"Life on the road?" repeated Tom, with raised eyebrows and a skeptical look on his lean face.

"Of course!" I countered, smugly. "Bands do a lot of performances on the road and all of the band directors can relate. Even though I would have to give the bus driver some credit for the inspiration, I would have to say it came off quite well. Besides it gave me an idea for the title of a new song I'm writing." With that I just smiled.

After a moment Cranky blurted through a frown, "Well! Are you gonna make us wait to hear the title?"

"I call it Bus Stop Blues."

The groans coming from Cranky and John were just barely overpowered by my cackling laughter.

SASQUATCH

I live in a part of the northwestern United States where there is a people, whose ways might not be as progressive as many others. This can be confirmed by the many rituals, dances, gatherings, traditional music, and beliefs in the supernatural exhibited by the local people. The people I am referring to are the folks of a little town called Lost Hollow in Washington State. Also living in the Northwest are Native Americans, but they seem to be a little more progressed than the Lost Hollow townsfolk. Except, of course, in the belief of a large creature that roams the great Northwest, called the Sasquatch. Lost Hollow townsfolk AND Native Americans all know of the existence of this mysterious creature. You might have heard the Sasquatch called some other name, such as Bigfoot. The Lakota Indians call it Chiye-tanka. Around the world these creatures are known by other names like Yeti, Yeren, and Yowie. Yowie probably got its name from the utterance of an unsuspecting miner or trapper.

We, in the Northwest all know it as the Sasquatch, but there is one who had not been convinced that Bigfoot ever existed. That is, until the opening day of fishing one year ago.

"Did you get those salmon eggs I told you about?"

"Yeah. I got a jar for each of us," replied John "Cranky" Cranklemeyer, sipping his coffee, and frowning.

I knew why Cranky was frowning. He was a purist fly-fisherman. Even though fly-fishing was my favorite fishing style, I was willing to use any back-up plan that would produce fish. And these special eggs were an almost guarantee.

"I talked to Tom and Sven this morning and they are all set," I said excitedly. "But Sven's a little nervous about going up to the north fork Stagomish River, right now."

Sven was the custodian at Lost Hollow High School who had come directly from Sweden at the age of 42. At the time, he didn't speak a word of English, but that was 30 years ago. Cranky taught P.E. at Lost Hollow and I was the school's band teacher.

"He's not worried about those Sasquatch reports, again, is he?"

"I'm afraid so. He wants bring his 30-06," I said.

The Whatcom County Tribune had printed a report by one of the farmers up at Arrowhead that indicated he stumbled upon a Sasquatch up by the North Fork a couple days ago. What the paper didn't report was that the farmer was poaching before opening day of fishing and also had an empty flask in his back pocket.

"I'm not letting him put that rifle in my truck," Cranky responded. "He'll probably get so spooked he'll shoot one of us with it! And there is no such thing as a Sasquatch, anyway."

The next morning Cranky pulled up to the front of my house in his brand new cherry red, crew-cab, short-bed, oversize-wheeled, 4x4, raised-up, get-down, 5.7 liter, V-8, fuel-injected, cruise-controlled, surround-sounded, fuel-guzzling pick-up truck.

"Wow, Cranky! What a beaut!" I exclaimed. "Maybe you oughta just leave that in your front yard so people can gawk at it. You sure you want to take that fishing?"

"Of course I do!" retorted Cranky, scowling. "I've gotta get my new ride broken in sometime, don't I?"

Where we were going I felt like Cranky could have left off the word "in" in the phrase, "broken in."

"Maybe we oughta take Tom's pick-up, Cranky. It's seen a lot of backcountry. I'd hate to see your new ride get a little scratch in it."

"Nonsense! I know how to drive on those back roads. Besides, my truck would feel a little more 'lived in' if it had a little scratch."

Forebodingly, I responded, "When you say 'little,' just how small would that 'little' be?

We stopped at the edge of town to pick up Sven. He was standing on his front porch next to a sleeping bag and pad, a large tackle box, and holding two long cases. As he walked up to the truck, Cranky gave him a suspicious look and asked, "What's in those cases, Sven?"

"Vell, dis vun hass my new eight und a haff foot fly rod," Sven replied, with a big ear-to-ear grin on his face.

Still looking suspicious, Cranky continued, "...and the other case?"

Sheepishly, Sven answered, "I tot ve might need sum protection."

"Sven, you've got yer 30-06 in there, don't you?"

"Vell, I vasn't plannink on takin' it uff da case."

"Sven! You take that right back into yer house. I'm NOT letting you put that weapon in my truck!"

"Vut about da Bigfoot efferybody hass been seein' up dere?" Sven looked worried.

"Those reports are a bunch of hogwash, Sven. There ain't no Sasquatch up where we're goin'."

I joined in, "Sven, there's four of us. No Sasquatch is going to get near four grown men."

After Sven put away his rifle we headed out to pick up Tom at his farm.

"So you don't believe in Bigfoot? I inquired of Cranky as the telephone poles whisked by.

"Sasquatch was probably invented by a bored Boy Scouts leader who got tired of hunting for Snipe," responded Cranky. "Have you ever noticed that most of the sightings were at night, by fishermen or hunters sitting around their campfires, drinking their hooch?"

"Vell, der VER dose sightings by Jimmy T'ornbush and Mrs. Gustafsson last montt," Sven retorted.

"You HAVE been out of the loop, haven't you?" stated Cranky, rhetorically.

"Vadya mean?"

Cranky asked, "Do you remember where Jimmy said he saw the Sasquatch?"

"Of course!" I responded. "He said he startled the Sasquatch behind his barn and the beast chased him all the way into the woods. That's why he didn't get home 'till after midnight. Jimmy musta been terrified."

"I doubt it," responded Cranky.

"Why?"

"The next day Sheriff Crowfoot went to the Thornbush barn and didn't find any Sasquatch tracks. But he DID find Jimmy's tracks. Crowfoot said the tracks didn't go into the woods, they went to Billy Middleton's front door. Seems Billy was having a card game at his house that night. Also seems that Billy got home late from that card game and made up that Sasquatch story because he knew he was in big trouble."

"Oh, that figures," I put in. "But what about the sighting by Mrs. Gustafsson?"

"Oh, yeah. Crowfoot visited her, too. The way she tells it, Mrs. Gustafsson was evidently serving dinner to her houseguests, which consisted of two space travelers from Alpha Centauri and a guy named Elvis Presley when the Sasquatch busted into her house demanding some of her cherry pie."

"Ohhhhh," I responded, looking down at the floorboards. If there was one positive thing that could be said about Mrs. Gustafsson, it was that she was one of the most creative people in Lost Hollow.

"So you see," continued Cranky, "there is a scientific reason for every sighting of this so-called Sasquatch. And I'm not about to start believing in all this hocus pocus about some man-like creature out in the woods. Mayor Eriksson was probably the one who started all these Sasquatch rumors, anyway, just to stir up some tourist dollars in Lost Hollow."

"You DO have to admit his story about prehistoric bones in Sanders pasture worked pretty well," I mentioned, grinning. Many considered Mayor Eriksson a tourism genius, even though his methods might be considered a little shady.

Cranky chuckled. "You're right. Paleontologists from all over this country showed up and were digging holes all over that pasture. That was the best business Mabel's Restaurant ever did."

"Und all da udder businesses, too!" Sven interjected.

"But the big windfall was that we didn't have to hire a digging company for our new sewer system," I added.

"Those scientists were pretty ticked when they found out that the bones they discovered in that pasture turned out to be elephant bones from Africa that were only two years old," Cranky continued. "Eriksson wasn't able to explain how they got there. I also found it interesting that the timing of the discovery of the hoax coincided with Mayor Eriksson's fishing trip to Alaska."

We all laughed out loud.

Soon, we pulled up to Tom's farmhouse. Of course, all of Tom's pets had to come out and greet us. I was surprised to see that Bear was loose. Bear was not really a bear. He just happened to be the largest dog in the county.

"No, Bear! Come back!" yelled Tom from the doorway of the barn.

"Go back, Bear!" I yelled from the passenger window.

But it was too late. Bear saw Cranky, and since Cranky was Bear's favorite human in the whole world, he bounded over to the driver's side of Cranky's truck. Bear heaved his huge frame up, standing on just his hind legs and put his paws on the driver's side door. As his paws slid down Cranky's door, there was the squealing sound of something scraping metal, not unlike the sound of fingernails scraping against a blackboard. Cranky and I got out of the truck and looked at that door. It had a beautiful, shiny, cherry-red paint job except for a pattern from top to bottom of four lines of missing paint on the left side and the four lines of missing paint on the right side.

"Bear! How could you?!!" This had come from Cranky as he was crushing his fishing hat with both hands. I looked at Bear, who had this ability of lying down on the ground with his paws over his head when he thought he had been caught doing something wrong. As pathetic as it was, he had this ability to illicit compassion from most humans. And it worked on Cranky.

"Oh, Bear!" blurted out Cranky, as he scratched him behind the ears.

As I stared at those huge scratches on Cranky's door and said, "Well, your truck now has that 'lived in' feel you were talking about."

As Cranky stared two holes into my forehead, Tom put his tackle into the bed of the truck and said, "The fish are waitin' you guys. Let's get cracking!"

After about an hour we hit the back-roads section of the forested area of the Cascades known as the Alpine Lakes. A light fog was beginning to roll in, making visibility at about 100 feet. Cranky was peering at the small road signs.

"Alright you guys. Keep yer eyes peeled for Forest Service Road 7203. Noticing one that veered off to the right, Cranky queried to Tom, "Does that sign say 7203?"

Tom, who was sitting in the front passenger side of the truck said, "Nope, it don't." Since I was sitting in the back seat, I wasn't a lot of help. However, as we went by that sign I noticed that the right half of it looked rotted away. We kept heading up the mountain for about another fifteen minutes.

Cranky, showing a mixture of frustration and anxiety on his face said, "I think we should have hit that road by now. You guys sure you haven't seen a road heading off to the right?"

"Hey look!" I exclaimed, pointing forward. "Is that it?"

"Where?"

I kept pointing forward and slightly to the left. "That's probably it!"

Cranky squinted, trying to focus on where my index finger was aimed. "That's not a Forest Service road, Cranky retorted. "That's a 4x4 trail."

Tom interjected, "That doesn't look wide enough for a 4x4 truck trail, but I think you oughta try it."

Cranky pulled up to the entrance of the so-called trail and stopped the truck. "Shouldn't there be a sign somewhere?" he asked.

Tom replied, "It's been a pretty tough winter and I read somewhere how the Forest Service is plannin' to replace a bunch o' signs this summer. I suggest you take this one but just go slow."

Cranky got back in and we headed down that track. As we lumbered along, Cranky was being careful, trying to miss the big holes in the trail and steer around the larger rocks. Cranky saw a fairly large stone on the left side of road and veered right while keeping his eye on that stone. Tom saw a huge branch jutting out from a fir tree, heading right for the right side of the truck.

"Uh, Cranky." But it was too late. The branch hit Cranky's right headlamp, smashing it inward, just before continuing along the side of the truck and making a squealing sound that reminded me of one of my beginning band clarinet players.

"Cranky, I wish you wouldn't do that," I shot forth with a frown. "I am trying to take a vacation here and not think about work." Cranky stopped the truck and we got out to inspect the damage. As suspected, halfway down the side of Cranky's truck there was an almost straight crease, without paint, running from front to back.

Sven exclaimed, "Cranky, yer right headlamp iss missink!"

As I was noticing that Cranky's hat was really durable, taking all that crushing and twisting by his powerful hands, I queried, "Maybe this isn't the forest road we want?"

"Of COURSE THIS IS NOT THE ROAD!" Cranky shouted. I was wondering how he made steam come off the top of his head like that.

"You, know, I wonder if that one road with the sign that was half rotted away might have been it?" I asked, glancing at Tom.

Tom replied, "Nope. That one said "72.""

"Didn't you say it was Road 7203, Cranky?" I quizzed. "It is possible that the last two digits of that sign were rotted off."

"Git in the truck," commanded Cranky. "We're goin' back."

Cranky was a pretty good driver and was able to drive in reverse and get us back to the logging road without hitting too many potholes or branches. We headed back down the road and came to the sign I had mentioned earlier. I got out and walked over to the sign and found the right half of it lying face-down next to the signpost. As I turned it over, a grin spread on my face and I held it up for my cronies to see. There were the numbers, "03."

Cranky yelled, "Get in! We've got to make up for lost time."

However, Tom jumped out and said, "Wait! I want you to take my picture next to Cranky's truck with the woods in the background." He thrust his camera into my hands and stood next to the left front fender.

"Wait a minute!" I called, handing the camera to Cranky and jumping out of the back seat. "I want in this, too!"

"Well, it's MY truck, so I'm going to be in the picture," Cranky retorted, shoving the camera into Sven's hands. The three of us stood there trying to look like mountain men as Sven snapped the picture.

When that was done, Cranky said, "Now let's get going. We've gotta make up for lost time!"

As we headed up that forest road I mentioned, "You might want to slow down a trifle, Cranky. This road looks like it hasn't had much maintenance lately."

Cranky, who was hunched over the steering wheel as if that would allow him to see farther into the fog, replied, "We wasted so much time on that wild goose chase that I'm trying to make up for lost time. I want to do a little fishing before we have to turn in tonight."

We watched as Douglas fir and hemlock trees whizzed past us in the fog. On every turn it seemed to me that we doing them on two wheels instead of four. After about eight of those hairpin lefts and rights, a creature bounded across the road from right to left directly in front of the car. Cranky swerved to his right, barely missing the animal, but catapulting the truck right into a bog. Fortunately, because of Cranky's oversized tires, the water didn't quite make it up to the door.

"Oh, great!" spouted Cranky, as he looked out the left and right windows. "Now how do I get out of this mess?"

"What was it that jumped out in front of you, a deer? I asked.

Tom said, "I thought it was a bear."

"It just looked like a blur to me," answered Cranky. "I was watching for rocks and holes in the road."

"I tot it vas runnink on it's hind legs," said Sven.

We all turned to look at Sven who was nervously peering out the back window.

"Now, Sven," began Cranky, scowling. "You aren't gonna start that Sasquatch business again, are you?"

"Vell, do bears run on der hind legs?"

The rest of us began nervously peering out the back window.

Tom said, "I th-think you might have been seeing things, Sven. That all happened so fast." But Tom did not take his eyes off the woods right behind us.

"Well one thing's fer sure, I interjected. "We can't spend the night in this truck. We've got to figure out how to get this thing out of the bog."

Cranky responded, "I've got a Come Along winch and cable in the back if we can find a tree close enough."

By opening the door and standing on the running rails, it was possible for Cranky to get to the truck bed without getting wet. Once he got the Come Along out of his tool box he turned and noticed that none of the rest of us had moved.

"Well!" he yelled. "Is someone going to help?!"

Grumbling, we all made our way back to the truck bed.

Holding the hardware in his hands and staring right at me he asked, "Who's going to take this cable to the bank?"

"Uh," I said intelligently, "uh these new boots haven't been broken in and the water would probably ruin 'em.

Cranky stared at Sven who had already started looking busy while attaching the cable to the rear of the truck. When Cranky turned to look at Tom he said, "Well!"

Tom replied, "I'm allergic to water."

"Allergic to WATER!?" Cranky responded, with squinted eyes.

"Yeah, I just found out about it this morning and…."

"Forget it!" Cranky retorted.

When Cranky made it to the bank, Tom called out supportively, "Your boots sure make a funny squeaky sound when they're all wet!"

Cranky yelled, "The only tree close enough is this one here." He was pointing at a little cedar that was only about a foot in diameter. I was a little doubtful that it would be strong enough to pull Cranky's 4 x 4 out of that mud.

"Have you connected that end to the tow hook underneath the truck, yet?" yelled Cranky as he started looping his chain around that tree.

Sven, who was holding the other end of the cable, was looking over the rear of the truck and said, "Unless somevun iss goink ta go unter vater ta hook dis cable on, I suppose dat vee cud just wrap it around dis bumper."

Once Cranky had his chain wrapped around the tree, he hooked it to the Come Along and started cranking the winch. The cable became taut and at first nothing happened. Then, as if in slow motion, the rear bumper began to bend outward. As one of the bolts holding the bumper popped out, Sven said, "Uh-oh!" But then, the truck gave a little shudder as if it were going to move. But then I saw something that gave my heart cause to pause.

"Uh, Cranky. You should stop," I said, anxiously.

"What?" yelled Cranky, as he continued to pump the crank.

"You should stop, now!" I yelled, fearfully.

"What?!" he yelled back as he pumped faster.

"STOP!" And he did. But too late.

The little tree, which I had noticed was tilting more and more towards the truck, started to topple. Sven, Tom and I stood transfixed by what we saw: a cedar tree falling straight for us.

Tom yelled, "Jump!" And we did. As Tom and Sven hit the water, I slipped and landed in the truck bed. The tree hit the cab dead center.

"Whoomp!"

When it hit, it bounced slightly to the right and fell next to the truck. In the process of falling beside the truck, it took off Cranky's right outside mirror, but more importantly, it took off the right rear passenger door, which Sven had left open.

I know, like me you're thinking it could have been worse; the tree might have hit my fishing tackle. But fortunately, Cranky's cab protected all my gear. When I let Cranky know my gear was ok, I would have sworn he was doing a victory dance. But why would he do that on his hat?

My thankfulness was short-lived, however. When the tree had hit the truck, it buried the truck about three inches deeper into the muck. This caused the water to begin flowing into the cab from where the missing door was. That was when I noticed that it was starting to get dark.

"Uh, Cranky?" But when people are in the middle of a victory dance it is very difficult to get them to come out of that trance-like state.

Tom, Sven and I decided we better grab the tent and bags and head to dry ground. It was fortunate that Cranky provided that tree for me to walk across because I never got wet. Since Cranky hadn't finished his victory dance, the rest of us put up the tent next to the bog.

We eventually got Cranky out of his reverie and we all crawled into our bags. The smell of the bog on my three friends' clothing was distracting to a sensitive guy like me. I guess they really didn't understand that, because when I asked them to sleep outside the tent they just made animal noises, caused smoke to come out of their ears and stayed right where they were.

Speaking of animal noises, have you ever slept outdoors in the woods? That's when you can hear sounds you don't normally hear during the daytime. Sven must have heard one of those sounds that the rest of us did not hear, because he said, "Listen! Did you hear dat?" We all got quiet. Even Cranky stopped his grumbling. Frankly, I didn't hear anything.

"There it is again!" Sven was cupping his hand to his ear. "Vat did yoo say dat animal vas dat jumped in front uff yer truck?"

"I really didn't see it, Sven," came Cranky's reply.

"I tink it's Him!" Sven declared, fixing each one of us with a wide eyed gaze. He looked so much like Boris Karloff in that old movie.

"Sven, have you ever seen Boris...."

"Listen!!" Sven was cupping his hand to his ear again. "I vish I had my rifle."

"Wait a minute, said Tom. "Is that an owl?"

Hearing something different I said, "I think that's a nighthawk."

Sven replied, "Or maybe it's da Bigfoot!"

Cranky responded, "Sven, there is no such thing." But Cranky was looking nervously at the door of the tent as he said that.

Here I must pause to give a little insight to the events that happened next. The local ranger was hiking down the mountain for his last check of his area, which included Forest Road 7203. he had gotten a late start and was hurrying down to his truck so he could head home. He had no flashlight with him, but he knew this road like the back of his hand. That is why he hit Cranky's downed tree with his shin. That tree wasn't across the road when he had gone up it earlier in the day. His howl would have wakened the dead and it certainly raised the hair on four fishermen!

The four of us jumped out of that tent faster than a squirrel being chased by a weasel. We all looked towards the direction of that horrendous sound. All we saw in the blackness of the night was some howling monster, jumping up and down near our downed tree. I figured that this Sasquatch was very angry that we toppled his favorite tree and probably wasn't in the mood to hear our apology, so I took off at a dead run downhill on the road. Sven, Cranky and Tom hearing me run must have guessed the wisdom of my thought process because they started screaming and were hard on my heels.

"Aaaaaah!" "Yowl!" "Eeeee!"

Hearing these inhuman sounds right behind me did not cause me to go any slower. We made it all the way down to the ranger station and probably had set a new record for cross-country running for people over the age of 30. Finding the station closed we sat on the porch, wheezing, perspiring, chests heaving, and not being able to talk. By the time we had some capacity for communication, the ranger had made it down to the station.

Cranky, still slightly wheezing, asked, "Did you (wheeze) just come down (wheeze) road 7203?"

"Yes, I did," came the ranger's response.

"I'm glad you are OK," said Sven. "Vee ver juust attacked up der by da Bigfoot!"

"He must be angry at something," said the ranger.

"YOU saw the Sasquatch?" Cranky asked.

"Well, I didn't exactly see him," said the ranger, "but I certainly heard him. He had some of the most unearthly screams and roars I have ever heard. Fortunately, he was running down the road, away from me."

"Yeah, I know!" I exclaimed. "He was chasing us all the way down the mountain."

"Yoo should put up a bevare of Bigfoot sign!" contributed Sven.

Needless to say, our fishing trip was cut short by the truck mishap. A couple of days later, Tom and I were standing outside of Henry's Automotive Repair, which was actually just an oversize garage where Henry did his trade. As we looked in to see the mud-caked, doorless, scratched-up, mirror-missing, headlamp-missing, cab-caved in, fenderless 4x4, I mentioned, "Well, at least it has more of that "lived-in" feel that Cranky was talking about."

Someone grunted just off to the side of us. We hadn't noticed the frowning Cranky sitting in his wife's Volkswagon, staring at the remains of his truck.

"When I asked Henry how much it was gonna cost to fix it up, he started laughing so long and loud I just gave up waiting in there."

Tom, in order to brighten up Cranky's day, walked over to the Volkswagon, reached into his back pocket and said, "Here, Cranky. I had this printed for you."

I peered over Tom's shoulder at the photo. There, in the picture, were the three of us with big grins, standing in front a beautiful cherry-red truck, which didn't look anything like the truck in Henry's garage. As Cranky looked at that truck in the picture, he started to put on a sad face, when he immediately looked surprised.

"What's that?" he exclaimed, pointing to something in the picture. Tom and I moved closer and looked to where he was pointing. In between Cranky and Tom, but back into the woods a ways, were two black eyes staring out from beside a bush. It was hard to make out facial features, but it almost looked like teeth were below those eyes... teeth in the shape of a smile. The three of us had a look of shock on our faces as Tom whispered, "Sasquatch."

THE SUBSTITUTE

Eventually, all schools require a specialist. This person is called the Substitute Teacher or Guest Teacher. Most students just call this person the "sub." A few refer to him or her as fresh meat.

As the band teacher for Lost Hollow High School, I was rarely sick and hardly ever needed a sub in my classes. This is probably due to my wife's cooking. Darla was an excellent housekeeper, seamstress, and gardener, but as a cook…well, let's just say she probably couldn't get a job at even the local fast food take-out joint. Don't get me wrong. I'm not complaining. No germ would ever get near her food, which is probably why I rarely got sick. However, there was one instance where I had to be gone from school and I was not looking forward to it.

"Well, Greg, are you looking forward to a day off of work?" This question was uttered by my friend Tom Brandston, just before taking a slurp of coffee. Tom, "Cranky" Cranklemeyer, and I were sitting in the corner booth at Mabel's café.

"If I was heading to my favorite fly-fishing hole I would probably say, 'yes'," I responded with a look of concern. "However, attending another of Darla's sister's weddings is not my idea of a "day off."

"Come on, Greg," a smiling Cranky interjected, "you get all that free food and get to party!"

"Do you know Darla's relatives?" I queried.

"I've met a couple," replied Cranky.

"I think there might be more reverie at the county morgue," I said. "Besides, I'm worried for the sub that's taking my place."

"There's always a sub somewhere in our school," countered Cranky. "The kids are used to having them."

I continued, "The band kids rarely get a sub and I'm not sure what might happen."

Tom asked, "Are you saying they might act up, switch instruments, throw paper airplanes and play wrong notes on purpose?"

With a look of surprise Cranky and I both stared at Tom.

Tom looked back at us sheepishly with a one-sided smile and remarked, "My nephew in Bellingham said that his band class did that once to a sub. Seems the sub ran out of the room and wouldn't come back."

"That's it! I'm not going!" I exclaimed, with a frown. "I can't do that to a sub."

"Nonsense!" Cranky countered, with a scowling glare at Tom. Tom dropped his gaze with a shrug. Cranky continued, "You just have to prepare the kids a little and they will be fine."

"So you want me to explain my expectation that they are conscientious, polite, and on task?" I responded.

"Absolutely not!" countered Cranky. "That's a waste of time. You have to use the Rumor Control technique.

"Rumor Control technique?" asked Tom.

The slight tilt of my head and expression on my face suggested that I wasn't quite sure about Cranky's new idea.

"Seriously," said Cranky, with a serious look on his face, "I started using it years ago and it works without a hitch."

"How does it work?" Tom asked.

"Well, you know that humans and students are often afraid of the unknown, right?" responded Cranky.

"Wait a minute, interjected Tom, frowning. "You just said humans AND students. Are you indicating that students aren't human?"

Cranky, frowning back, answered, "That all depends on whether or not there's a sub in the room." He continued, "As I was saying, kids are afraid of the unknown. So, you just start little scary rumors about the incoming sub so that fear will squelch any plan by the kids to act up."

With that statement, Cranky sat back in the booth with his hands behind his head and an impish smile across his lips.

"And just how do I get those rumors started?" I asked.

"You just accidentally let slip little tidbits about the sub to some of the more "gossipy" students. If you start early enough, the stage will be set for your absence. I stared at my coffee cup, contemplating, as Mabel brought our breakfast.

"I wouldn't say he's mean, Jimmy, just a little eccentric."

It was the end of the school day and I was putting away music in a file drawer. Jimmy Thornbush, one of the school's trumpet players, was standing in the doorway of my office, with his trumpet case in hand. We were discussing the guest teacher who would be taking my place in a few days.

"What does that word mean, Mr. Olson? 'Eccentric'."

"It just means that he doesn't do things like other people," I responded.

"Like how?" Jimmy asked.

"Well, for example, his baton is different than mine. His has a D.E.D. installed."

"A 'D.E.D.'?"

"Yeah, that stands for Dart Expulsion Device. You know how most teachers just remind rowdy kids to stop talking or stop distracting others. The EXTERMINATOR just aims his baton at the kid and fires."

With a look of horror, Jimmy exclaimed, "He's called the EXTERMINATOR?!"

"Only by students. NEVER call him that to his face." Jimmy looked like he had to go pee.

Smiling, I said, "Well, Jimmy, it was nice chatting with you. I have to head home, now. Have a good evening!" As I left Jimmy standing in the hallway with his eyes wide open, I felt a slight tinge of guilt but still headed out of the building with an ear-to-ear grin on my face.

The next morning I was dusting off the shelf next to Ragweed's cubicle in the band storage room. Ragweed, who was placing his clarinet on the rack, had gotten his nickname from the effect he had on me whenever he attempted to play his clarinet. I think I am allergic to those kinds of sounds. His real name is Barney Wertelmeyer

"I just hope he's not wearing black!" I continued.

"Whadya mean, Mr. Olson?" asked Ragweed as he slid his clarinet onto the shelf.

I continued, "Whenever he wears black, that means he is in a bad mood. One day when he was wearing black he pulled out a bazer and used it on one of the unruly kids."

"Whadya mean, bazer?"

"It's a new device used for crowd control," I replied.

"Do you mean like a taser?"

"No. No. It's much worse."

"What's it do?" Ragweed asked, the concern written on his face.

"It's too horrible to describe. In fact, I don't even want to think about it. You'll be ok if she's not wearing any black," I replied.

"I thought you said it was a 'he'."

"It depends on the disguise," I responded, squinting my eyes and looking right and left as though I was concerned about eavesdroppers. Ragweed now stared at me with a look of awe.

He queried, "Disguise?"

"Yeah. I heard that he's a master of disguise. And if he comes as a little ol' lady, watch out!"

Ragweed half closed his eyes, looking at me with a wry smile and responded, "Really."

Noticing the distrust, I redirected the conversation. "I also heard he has this big black bag he brings with him. Just hope he never reaches into it."

Now looking a little more concerned, Ragweed asked, "Why? What's in it?"

"His tools."

"What's so scary about tools?" Ragweed questioned.

"Barney, those aren't mechanic's tools. Those are crowd control tools. And no matter what, if he brings out the "star," just get up and run!" I exclaimed, conjuring up a look of fear.

"Run because of a star?" Ragweed was starting to look a little more uncomfortable.

I looked from side to side to indicate to Ragweed that I wanted to make sure no one was listening. I said, "Have you ever seen any of those kung fu & karate movies?"

"Whoa!" exclaimed Ragweed. "Don't you think the principal would bar someone like from teaching in our school?"

"Why? Mr. Moss has the best controlled classes of any substitute teacher."

"His name is Mr. Moss?" Ragweed asked as he headed for the door.

"That's right, Barney. That is, if he isn't in disguise."

Ragweed stopped and responded, "And what is his name if he IS in disguise."

"I don't remember, Barney, but I think it starts with a 'Q'."

As Ragweed left the room I noticed the inside part of his eyebrows had lifted up and his eyes were opened wide. I tried to keep a straight face but couldn't keep the corners of my lips from curling up slightly.

The day before I was to be gone I was in the faculty room at lunch, sitting next to Cranky.

"Did you say a Mrs. Quagmire is to be your sub?" Cranky asked.

"That's right," I responded, smiling.

"I don't remember her. Is she from around here?" Cranky asked.

"Nope," I responded. "She's from Anacortes. The last time she subbed out here was about two years ago. But she's still in the sub pool."

Cranky asked, "Why did you want her for your sub?"

"She is short and timid."

You aren't worried about your class getting out of control?"

"Nope. And just to make sure I called her and told her to bring that big black tote she sometimes uses and her baton."

"What will THAT do?" Cranky asked, with a puzzled look on his face.

"THAT," I replied smiling, "will be the frosting on the cake."

Cranky just shook his head as we got up from the table to head back to class.

The next day, Darla and I headed to Mount Vernon for the wedding of her sister, Dolly. I won't bore you with the details but it was about as much fun as watching a cube of butter melt in a pan of cold water. Being in my band room would have certainly been more interesting.

"Did you hear about the sub?" asked Jimmy, who was standing in the center of the band room.

"Yeah," responded Blap, who was one of our band's tuba players. "They call him the EXTERMINATOR."

"Oh, no! I've heard of him," Jimmy squelched.

"It's not a HIM," interjected Priscilla, who played flute. "I was just in the office to get an absence slip and Mr. Olson's sub was there talking to the secretary. It was a she."

With a concerned look Blap asked, "What did she look like?"

Priscilla looked quizzically at Blap and replied, "She's just a little ol' grey-haired lady."

With a look of horror Jimmy let out a gasp. "It's worse than I thought," he said. "He's in disguise!"

Ragweed, who had come in to the band room in time to hear the comment about the EXTERMINATOR, joined in, "Priscilla what color of clothes was she, er, he wearing?"

"Mrs. Quagmire was dressed in all black."

The three boys yelped in unison, "Mrs. Quagmire!!"

Squeamishly, Jimmy squeaked, "That starts with the letter 'Q'."

The four kids looked at each other with disconcerting looks upon their faces, along with all the other kids who had circled around to hear the conversation. Since the rumors had already been flowing through the school for days, all the kids had the same looks of trepidation.

Just then, the door to the band room began to open slowly. Everyone froze. It seemed like it took minutes for that door to open all the way, but it was probably only a few seconds. And then, walking slowly through the opening, came a terrifying figure. Oh sure, it looked like a little ol' lady, but the kids knew better. She looked like she wasn't even 5 feet tall, with a medium short quaff of silvery hair, rounded spectacles, and a black shawl over a black blouse, which was tucked into a floor-length black skirt.

The little lady stopped in the doorway and slowly scanned the band room from right to left until her eyes rested on the group of kids. Her eyes locked onto the band kids like a heat-seeking Sidewinder missile. The students were completely frozen where they stood, staring with mouths agape at the figure in the doorway. Slowly, her mouth opened and with a smile she said, "Would you mind taking a seat?"

With a sound of rushing wind, the last student got to his seat in 2.2 seconds. As the students watched the little woman slowly make her way to the front of the room, their eyes fell upon the black tote she was carrying in her right hand. No one had noticed it when she was standing in the doorway. She hoisted it onto the piano, which was in the front of the room.

She turned to look at 23 motionless kids and said, "We might be able to make more music if you had your instruments out."

There was a split-second pause as the kids turned to look at each other. And then, with another rush of wind, every kid had his or her instrument out, ready to go.

"My name is Mrs. Quagmire," she began in a high-pitched scratch. "I will be your guest teacher for the day." The class looked at each other with nervous expressions around.

"Why don't we begin with the warm-up number 13 in your book," she continued. One of the clarinet players in the front row started playing some notes to see if her reed was working. Mrs. Quagmire noticed it and began to reach into her black bag. The kids all watched as her right hand slid into the bag. Ragweed began to perspire. As quick as a flash, Mrs. Quagmire whipped out her baton and aimed it at the clarinet player who was warming up. The first two rows of musicians hit the floor.

Mrs. Q smiled at the clarinet player and intoned, "I think it would be better if we played the warm-up together, don't you?" With a very serious look, the clarinetist just simply nodded agreement from underneath his chair.

Once the band members had regained their chairs, Mrs. Q had them play the warm up. When they were finished she paused, looking at each member of the band.

She asked, "Are you sure you were playing number 13?" The students just looked at each other, nodding.

"I just remember it sounding differently last time I heard it," she remarked. "I see in Mr. Olson's lesson plans that he has you next playing The Thunderer by the great John Philip Sousa. Let's try that!"

Blap looked at Jimmy with a nervous glance and swallowed. The Thunderer was pretty difficult and sounded....well, lets just say that Charlie's Machine Shop had sounds closer to the authentic original. When the band stopped playing at the end of the song, Mrs. Q put down her baton and stared. She then reached into her bag and said, "It looks like you need some help playing the right rhythms." Out came a black rectangular shaped electronic device, which she aimed at the percussion section. Two of them yelped, and ran straight out of the room. Mrs. Quagmire stared at the swinging door.

"Obviously, those kids aren't used to using a metronome," she intoned, as she turned back to the music. "We probably need to have each section work on this separately. Let's start with the percussion section," she offered as she smiled her 'little-ol-lady' smile at the last row. "From the top! And-a-one-and-a-two..."

The percussion section endeavored to do the best they could. The rest of the band was pretty impressed. It was obvious that they were focusing because instead of sounding like a train wreck, they sounded more like an avalanche. Still, when they were done the band looked at Mrs. Q to see what her reaction would be.

At first she just stood there, looking intently without expression at the percussion section. The band waited, nervously. Then, she quietly remarked, "It is obvious that you deserve this." Then she slowly reached into that ominous black bag. As her hand slowly reached all the way down into the bottom of that huge container, percussionists began to perspire. Ragweed licked his lips. Jimmy felt his mouth go dry. Blap's mouth just hung open.

She started fumbling around for a few seconds but then had obviously found what she was looking for because she began to smile and slowly bring her arm out of that bag.

"Aha!" she exclaimed, which caused Ragweed to rise two inches from his chair.

At first, she brought her arm out slowly, but then flung her hand high in the air.

"You need this!" she exclaimed, brandishing a huge gleaming star above her head.

Every eye in the room looked upon that instrument of dread. Every mouth dropped three inches. Every vocal cord vibrated to the pitch of a double high c, and at that moment the room emptied itself of every human except for Mrs. Quagmire.

As she stared confusingly at the door and open windows, she said aloud, "I wonder why they were afraid of the gold star I was going to give the percussion section for trying so hard?" As she looked at the star in her hand, she commented, "I realize it's only cardboard, but it's the thought that counts."

Mrs. Quagmire put her baton and "tools" away in her bag and headed for the door, thinking that the bell must have rung. "My hearing is not what it used to be," she thought.

As she reached for the light switch she thought, "What an obedient, responsive class. They seemed to hang on my every word." Just before closing the door she looked around the room and said aloud, "Maybe I should substitute here more often."

GRIM REAPER

"Ok, students. You have been bugging me for a long time to take a major trip, so here it is. We are going to the Funtimes Theme Park!"

At first, the kids just stared at me, waiting for the punch line and trying to read my expression. They were good at that by now. Maybe that was because of the various events that I had planned for them in the past; events like the Happy Fair, where they could make me happy by dusting the instrument cabinets, or organizing the sheet music. There was also Mr. Olson's Wonderland, where they could win prizes for the most music stands tightened or most chalkboard space cleaned. I suppose their skepticism was mostly developed during the time when I took them for a "band trip" to the school grounds to pull weeds.

"Mr. Olson," blurted trumpeter, Jimmy Thornbush, whose hooded eyes indicated he wasn't entirely convinced I was on the level. "Are we going to have to clean the gum off the bottom of the chairs again?"

"Or tape the sheet music?!" yelled an outspoken percussionist in the back.

"Or clean the walls?!" piped up Tommy, who played tuba and whose nickname was Blap.

"Wow, you guys," I countered, "I hadn't even thought of those things. Thanks for giving me some ideas, heh, heh." But the class was not laughing with me. In fact, the way they were looking at me made me a little uneasy. I wondered if this was how Captain Bligh felt just before that infamous mutiny.

But as I have said in other situations, timing is everything.

"Look!" I exclaimed, while grabbing a brochure off of my director's stand and holding it aloft. I was pointing at the colorful, glossy picture on the front of the brochure, which showed kids sitting in a roller coaster car, with their hair flying back and smiles (or grimaces) on their faces. Right above the picture was the advertisement, "FUNTIMES THEME PARK - Where your day starts with FUN!" Evidently, this must have given credence that I was on the level, because in a few seconds my students were cheering and giving high-fives.

As I looked around the room, everyone was animated, smiling and talking excitedly about this new event. I saw, in the middle of it all, a hand go up. The hand belonged to a very prim and proper flute player named Priscilla, who has the record for most the consecutive days without talking out of turn. After I quieted the kids down, I called on Priscilla.

"Mr. Olson, how are we going to pay for this field trip?" Priscilla asked. Instantly, there was complete silence, with 76 eyes staring at me. I can't tell you how many times the practical Priscilla has stumped me with a question that I can't answer. Questions like, "How do you trill a double high Bb?" or "Am I in tune?" or "How do you make the drummers play softer?" Actually, I have the answer to the last one: "Just put sheet music in front of them and have them try to sight-read it..heh, heh." But I was already prepared for Priscilla's latest question.

"Priscilla," I responded, "Funtimes Theme Park is installing a new ride and wants a band to play for its grand opening. My brother-in-law works for Funtimes and suggested us. So, Funtimes will pay for the bus to take us and give us each a free pass for unlimited rides that day." I think you could have heard a pin drop in the band room at that moment. That's what happens when 38 jaws are hanging wide open in my room. I didn't have much time to enjoy the silence because in just a few seconds the cheering, high fives, and now the tooting of horns grew tumultuous. I had to enjoy the celebration, though, especially with shouts of "Mr. Olson, you rock!" and "Awesome, Mr. Olson!" and "Mr. Olson is the greatest band director alive!" The student who said that last thing got an A+ that day.

When that special day arrived, the kids all loaded into the bus and I made sure everybody had their instruments and music; except for Ragweed. Whenever Barney Wertelmeyer, alias Ragweed, forgot his clarinet, I considered that a good day. Ragweed had the ability to cause my asthma to flare up whenever he made sounds on his instrument. Maybe someday Ragweed will turn those sounds into music. But alas, someday was not here yet, Ragweed remembered his clarinet and the busload of students and director headed for Funtimes.

As always, Ragweed liked to sit up front where he could pester, er, converse with the band director. "Mr. Olson," continued Ragweed on his fourteenth question so far, "what's the name of the new ride at Funtimes Theme Park?"

"Ragwee…, er, Barney, it's called the Grim Reaper."

"Wow!" interjected Jimmy. "Do you think it's dangerous?"

"I don't know the first thing about it, Jimmy. But it's got to be safe enough for them to let the public on it." I'm not so sure I actually believed my last remark. "I doubt if we will really have time to ride it because I hear the lines will be pretty long for this new ride. They're expecting to create a new attendance record with this Grand Opening."

"Oh," Jimmy replied, with a saddened look on his face.

I knew the kids were looking forward to this ride. But the reality was that once we finished playing our special music for this event the park was due to be packed, with most of the public wanting to jump onto the newest torture…er…experience the Park had in store for them.

Once we arrived and unloaded, a man in a tuxedo came over to me and stuck out his hand. As I took it he said, "Mr. Olson, I am so glad you were able to play for us. My name is James Burke, and I am the General Manager of Funtimes."

I replied, "I am glad we could come." I guess I was glad for the kids, but personally would rather be standing in the middle of the Stagomish River with a fly pole in hand. I was not one for doing the rides. They always made me queasy.

I got the band kids in position next to the front entrance and even though it was twenty minutes before the opening of the park, a huge crowd was gathering. Pretty soon we started playing marches and pep songs for the crowd. They must have been in a good mood because they actually applauded our numbers. Finally, Mr. Burke signaled that he was ready to give his speech. I won't bore you with the details about how Funtimes was honored to provide entertainment for families, loved children and because of that love was committed to providing new experiences like the new ride. Somehow, I must have missed the part where Funtimes was glad to make a lot of money from these children.

Burke finished his speech and the audience, which already looked to be at about a thousand, politely applauded, thankful that that the speech was short. As he walked up to the ribbon, which was stretched across the main entrance, he turned to the audience while holding an extra large pair of scissors. He announced while pointing his scissors my way, "Could we also give a big thanks to the Lost Hollow Band, under the direction of Greg Olson!" The audience gave a nice round of applause and as it died down Burke continued, "And to show our appreciation, Funtimes is going to let the band be the first to ride the Grim Reaper!"

As my band was cheering, Burke was saying something I could hardly make out. But I thought I heard something about the band director taking the inaugural ride. I tried to get Burke's attention but he had already cut the ribbon and was leading the way to the new ride. I hadn't seen the Grim Reaper yet but I was fairly confident that no one was going to get THIS band director on THAT.

As the crowd flooded through the large main opening to Funtimes, my students put away their instruments in their cases and I led them into the park. As we headed toward the center of the park, Ragweed-of-a-thousand-questions began interrogating me about the Grim Reaper.

"How high…"

"How fast…"

"How long…"

"How safe…"

I was getting frustrated by being pummeled by the many questions for which I did not have the answer when I noticed the entire band behind me had stopped and were looking up to the sky. I faced forward again and saw the blinking neon sign, which was about twenty feet across, flashing, "THE GRIM REAPER," in an angry red color. Also lit up next to the words was the painted twenty-foot tall figure in a robe, holding a long-handled scythe and pointing a skeletal finger right at me.

That was disconcerting enough but what I saw next made me want to relieve my bladder. Right behind the sign was a scary form. It was wearing the same robe that I had seen on the sign, while holding a …hopefully fake…scythe. The scary part was the fact the form was facing me and wiggling his index finger, indicating that I should come forward.

But I didn't move because right behind the form was the most terrifying structure that man has ever built. There was a silvery ten-foot metal cylindrical tube with a window in the front and a window in back. On the side of this box was a hinged door, with the hinges on top allowing the door to open up. This tube was attached to a long snake-like arm, which seem to come out of the heavens above because it was so tall, I could hardly make out where it ended. Hardly visible was another cylindrical box that I estimated was at least 100 feet in the air or maybe deep into a cumulous cloud, held up by a second snake-like arm. I was not sure exactly what happened when this machine did its business but I WAS sure it would be doing it without me!

As my thoughts were coming back to earth, I tuned into Burke, who was saying to the audience, "...and now the first ride goes to Mr. Olson, Director of the Lost Hollow Band!" His arm was extended my way with an upturned hand as though he was offering his favorite dish to a ravenous dinner crowd. He could have just as easily said, "And now here is the roast duck ala orange that you have been waiting for!"

I was earnestly shaking my head and saying, "Oh, no, I couldn't possibly take the honor away from my band students..."

"Nonsense, Mr. Olson," came the reply from Burke. "You are their leader and should certainly be the first."

As I looked around at my students, they were all nodding their affirmations, and began "helping" me to that hinged door. Holding the door was the attendant, whom I assumed was human, wearing a robe and holding a scythe. As much as I struggled, there were so many students moving towards the "monster" ride that I couldn't stop the momentum. As I inched closer to that box of terror I turned to see Burke grinning from ear-to-ear. His smile looked more like the grin from a hungry wolf.

When I was halfway through the door some student yelled, "If you let go of the door frame, Mr. Olson, it would be easier for us to help you in!" Somehow, even with my struggling, I found myself being strapped into the chair with one of those five star straps that pilots wear. Then someone wrapped Velcro straps, which were attached to the seat, around my legs.

I queried, "Aren't these straps a bit much for this ride?"

Just outside the door I heard Burke's voice. "You'll need those straps for the rolls, spins and upside-down maneuvers!"

"Whaa....!" But just then the door closed.

If you would have looked inside the window at that moment you would have a seen a wild apparition, with arms flinging, jaw moving, and eyes bugged out.

"Wow!" exclaimed Ragweed. "Mr. Olson sure is excited about going on that ride!"

"Yeah," replied Jimmy, with a slightly dejected look on his face, "I wish it was me."

I won't bore you with the details of how the Grim Reaper's arm began a slow rotation, allowing me to see the clouds that I thought I would be entering, or the momentum of its downward "fall," or the way the tube rotated and spun, or the loud sounds that accompanied the ride.

"I didn't know Mr. Olson could scream that loud!" yelled Blap.

"Oh yeah he can." Jimmy responded. "You should have heard him in beginning band when the trumpets tried to play their first notes!"

Finally, during one of my prayers asking God to take me quick, the ride jerked to a halt. The fact I was at the highest point of the ride and was upside down was not a concern at first. I was just glad the monster had stopped moving. But after five minutes, with most of my blood probably pooling in my head, I was wondering what was taking so long. I could see through the upper part of the front window that there was a huge crowd looking up at me.

A man was rapidly hitting buttons on the control panel of the Grim Reaper when Burke came up to him with a concerned look on his face. "What's wrong, Mike?" Burke asked.

Mike replied, "I don't know, Mr. Burke. One moment it was fine and then it just stuck. I'm guessing it's a software problem."

Burke frowned and moved closer to Mike so that the crowd couldn't hear him. "You've GOT to get this thing working or else we stand to lose thousands of dollars," Burke hissed.

"Ok, Mr. Burke. Right away!"

As Mike quickly opened a panel on the back of the controller, Burke faced a concerned-looking audience.

"Nothing to worry about folks; just a little software glitch that Mike will have fixed in a jiffy. But to help you wait, Funtimes is giving free ice cream to everybody waiting!" A huge cheer went up from the students as Burke led them to the ice cream parlor.

While I was sitting upside-down in the G. R.'s pod, I noticed it starting to get dark. Then I observed all of my audience walking away, following a small figure whom I assumed to be Burke. Then the lights went out. I said to myself, "They've left me here and shut down the ride!"

Then I said, "Get hold of yourself, Olson. There is no way that Burke or your students would just leave you here, right?"

After taking a moment to think about it rationally, I started screaming uncontrollably.

"Don't leave me!"

"Come back!"

"Arrgh!"

When my screaming and arm waving brought no results and my voice was basically gone, I started trying to figure out what to do. Since it was obvious they weren't coming back I tried to figure out how to get out and off of the contraption. The first thing, of course, was to get myself right side up. I looked at my five-point seatbelt and saw a little button right in the middle where al the straps met. I pushed it.

The next thing I remember was hanging upside down by my legs with my head about one inch from the ceiling (which was now the floor). I had forgotten about the Velcro straps around my legs. As I was trying to reach the straps I was reminded that I probably shouldn't have had that last helping of Mabel's pecan pie. By grabbing the seat belt I was able to reach one of the straps and yank on it. I was free of it and now hanging by ONE strap around my right leg. This was a little harder to get to and took me a number of tries to get it released. But finally, I grabbed the strap and with the help of shear gravity I was able to release the hold on me. Of course, I landed in a heap on the roof of the little compartment.

I got on my hands and knees and stared out the little window into space and some beautiful twinkling stars. It was then that I realized that I had no idea how I was going to get down from this high-altitude monster. I looked at the door and saw a red handle next to the words, "EMERGENCY EXIT." I pulled it.

The door flung open, pulled down by gravity and I was staring about a hundred feet out and down to ants walking around the ground. However, those ants where wearing hats, talking into cell phones and pointing in my direction. Just then the lights came back on.

The first thing I noticed that should have indicated my imminent danger was the whirring sound of machine wheels and cogs engaging and making metallic sounds. The next thing was the movement of my little compartment. It began to roll.

I began to become elated, thinking that finally I can get off this beast when I realized that my seatbelt was not on and the door was…OPEN!

As the pod continued rolling, I started rolling, too, right toward the open door! I reached out, trying to grab at something to help me stop rolling and latched onto the seatbelt. That was somewhat comforting except that my feet were now dangling out of the open door.

There was a huge gasp from the growing crowd below. Most of the crowd was holding ice cream cones and pointing in my direction. Someone screamed.

"You're right!" exclaimed Blap to Jimmy, just before taking a lick of his pistachio-licorice-blueberry cone. Mr. Olson really CAN scream loud.

"Yup," Jimmy replied, as he licked his peanut butter, lemon meringue, watermelon ice cream cone. I would say he is the loudest screamer in Whatcom county, maybe even in Washington State!

As the screaming continued and I was becoming hoarse, the Reaper's arm swung down, causing the pod to become right side up. I fell into the chair and the door slammed shut. The Grim Reaper slowed to a stop at ground level and Mike opened the door. When he saw the apparition standing in the doorway he said, "Wow, Mr. Olson, you look a little like Death warmed over!"

"That gives me an idea!" exclaimed Burke, who was standing next to the Grim Reaper's door. He grabbed the scythe from the attendant and gave it to me. Turning to the reporters he said, "Now there's a picture for you. The Grim Reaper rides the Grim Reaper!"

Flashes started popping right and left, startling me out of my stupor. I raised my hands to shield my eyes, dropping the scythe and falling back into the pod's chair. The scythe fell over, striking the control panel's big black button. There was the whirring sound of machine wheels and cogs engaging…

A couple of days later, as Jimmy was nearing the front door of the school, he saw a small huddle of kids standing off to the side.

"Hey, you guys, whatcha doin'?"

Priscilla replied while holding up the front page to the Whatcom County Tribune," Look, Jimmy. Mr. Olson made the front page!"

In the large picture Jimmy saw a very disheveled form, holding a scythe and standing in the doorway of the Grim Reaper. The headline stated, "LOCAL BAND TEACHER MAKES EXCITING INAUGURAL FLIGHT!"

Blap said, "That's so cool that Mr. Olson got to ride it twice!"

"Actually," Jimmy countered, "you can hear Mr. Olson riding it every day."

"What?!" Ragweed exclaimed.

Jimmy continued, "Mr. Burke up at Funtimes thought that Mr. Olson's screams added a nice touch to the ride. So he got the video from one of the reporters and got the audio off it. Now, every time someone rides it they hear Mr. Olson's screams."

"Ooh, that's kinda eerie," Priscilla replied.

"That's the whole idea!" responded Jimmy. It adds just the right amount of fright to the Grim Reaper."

Ragweed asked, "Do you think Mr. Olson will ride it again?"

"I doubt it," replied Blap. "When I delivered the paper to his house, Mrs. Olson said he won't get into a car or anything that moves."

"Well, I certainly hope he gets over that by next month!" Priscilla urged. "My dad is the chief engineer on that bridge project over at Diablo Canyon that gets done in twenty days. We are supposed to play for the opening ceremony."

Ragweed offered, "He'll probably be OK by then."

"I suppose I shouldn't tell him about the bungee jumping." Priscilla said apprehensively.

"Bungee jumping?" asked Blap, with raised eyebrows.

Priscilla responded, "My dad's company is offering free bungee jumping for the occasion."

"How cool!" exclaimed a smiling Ragweed.

"My dad was going to encourage Mr. Olson to be first to jump," concluded Priscilla, with slight uneasiness in her voice. "Maybe we shouldn't tell him about that."

The kids all looked at each other with concern.

"Don't tell 'im!" they all said at once.

SUMMER CAMP

One of the reasons I go hiking in the woods is for solitude. It's great to get away from the rumbles, honks, pings, slams, jingles, and rattles, not to mention the many sounds that AREN"T from the beginning band. I just find that the woods are my seclusion from the troubles and sounds of the regular world.

"So how is it, Greg, that you find yourself in the woods with a BAND!" I asked myself, rhetorically. Not hearing an answer, I continued on the road to Last Lake Summer Camp. Actually, there had been an answer to that question in the form of a request from the wife.

"I want a new TV by September, Greg Olson! One that actually works!"

That meant I would actually have to work this summer instead of spending half of it fishing and the other half, angling. I know what you're thinking, that the words 'fishing' and 'angling' mean the same thing. They are quite different, however. 'Fishing' means that you are putting a line in the water in the pretense of trying to pull something with fins out of it. 'Angling,' on the other hand, means trying to find ways to postpone something undesirable, like cleaning gutters, mowing the lawn, vacuuming the house, and the like. Angling can include having to go to Mabel's for an important breakfast meeting with Tom and Cranky. It can also mean having to go down to the local hardware store to see about that part for the lawn mower, but discovering that a new shipment of fishing poles has come in. It can also mean driving your car to see if that latest tire alignment is working, even though your golf clubs are in the trunk and the straightest road runs right by the golf course.

"I think my car pulls to the right," I would say. "I think I'll just go check it out."

"Are your golf clubs in the car?" would be the response from the kitchen, even though it usually would be a few seconds too late.

Of course, 'angling' CAN mean fishing. A statement like "Well, I'm off to go catch our dinner, hon," will bring such fits of laughter that you'll be out the door and to the fishing hole before the wife can even come up with the list of chores.

However, this particular summer I had to make some money for Darla's new TV. That's why I signed up to be an instructor at Last Lake Summer Camp. It must have gotten its name from the fact that you go for miles and miles and miles and miles up this mountain, and just before you get to the pinnacle you hit the lake - almost literally. As you just crest the last rise, the lake is right there, with a hairpin turn in the road to the right to avoid an early morning bath. Having already showered, I decided to take the right and pull into the camp's parking area. As I got out of the car and immediately smelled the pines, I had the thought, "Isn't this a beautiful place?"

"Well?" came a voice into my thoughts. "I asked if this was a beautiful place."

I turned to see Priscilla Pukswankle, who was a flutist in my high school band and one of the camp counselors. "Yes, Priscilla," I responded, "this lake is gorgeous."

"Your cabin is all ready, Mr. Olson," Priscilla said. "You'll be bunking with three other teachers."

"With?" I asked, slightly surprised. "I thought we each got our own cabin."

Priscilla laughed, "We don't have THAT many cabins, Mr. Olson. You're such a kidder!"

As I followed Priscilla to the building in which I would be sleeping for the next two weeks, I noticed the other buildings, all of which were built of logs. There was a larger one near the lake, which I assumed was the headquarters. Lined up in a neat row on the beach were some canoes and one of those watercraft that you pedal.

"When do the kids arrive, Priscilla?" I asked.

"They'll be coming in tomorrow, Mr. Olson. Today we are having the organizational meetings in that building," she said while indicating the large structure with her index finger. "That's also the Mess."

"Well, then. Somebody should clean it up before the kids arrive!" I stated, indignantly.

Priscilla laughed. "Oh, Mr. Olson. You're such a kidder! That's the Mess Hall, where everybody eats." Feeling slightly ignorant, I followed Priscilla to my cabin with fewer comments.

"People," continued Pete Arnold, the camp director, "those are all of the instructions for the camp except for one last thing. On the east side of the lake there's a trail that goes down the mountain. There are red ribbons tied around many of the trees there. Those ribbons and the sign there are a warning that no one should go any further down that path!"

"Why is that?" I asked, with concern.

"There is a mama bear with cubs in a den down that way," Pete responded. "She's just a black bear and doesn't come up this way. I think she is terrified of some of the sounds we create up here." There was some laughter from the counselors.

"Just make sure no kids go that way," Pete said, with a serious look on his face, which seemed even more serious as his eyes locked onto mine.

The first day was an exciting day, with the arrival of a couple of buses full of middle school kids, loaded up with instrument cases, suitcases, pillows, and a lot of smiles and laughter. I was enjoying the arrival and was beginning to think doing summer camp was all right. All the students got placed into various cabins and were told to stow their belongings. Each cabin's inhabitants had to decide on a group name before lunch, however. On the way into lunch they brought signs indicating their decisions. There were the Wolverines, Bumblebees, Falcons, Hornets, and others. The group that sat closest to me voted to be the Sea Snakes. I am not sure how this particular mascot ended up at camp, seeing as how it had nothing to do with the Northwest and certainly nothing to do with mountains. But it was certainly better than the next table's choice of the Klingons. I was told this name came from a war-like race of aliens in some science fiction TV episode. Judging by their table manners, it was a well-chosen mascot.

"Boys and girls," began Pete Arnold. "Welcome to Last Lake Band Camp! There are a few things I would like you to know...." As Pete continued on, I took in the Mess Hall. It was a very large room with huge, wooden beams stretching above us. The walls were beautiful logs, which ran the entire distance of the room. The tables were also very long, with long wood benches upon which all of the camp was sitting. At one end was the kitchen and at the other was the stage, upon which stood Pete Arnold.

"...and after classes you will have free time.....," he continued.

I drifted out of Pete's speech again, running aground on a beautiful daydream. I was imagining being on a secluded section of a stream, fly-pole in hand, the sun on my face, and birds singing in the trees. The birds were somewhat out-of-tune, however, as I came out of my daydream to hear the kids singing a camp song, led by director, Pete.

"The other day, I met a bear,
A great big bear,
Oh way out there......"

There could have been maybe fifty other songs they could have sung which would have made me feel a little more at ease. It went on.....

"And so I ran
Away from there
But right behind
Me was that bear."

The singing of that song, so soon after the speech yesterday about that momma bear, made me a little uncomfortable. Or maybe it was that hard, wooden bench I was sitting on.....

The rest of the day was spent directing the band, teaching guitar classes, and some private lessons. Others handled the 'activities' - boating, hiking, horseback riding, and the like. Throughout my day, that daydream of the fishing stream kept coming back and I wondered if there might be a time where I could get away. I figured that since my last class finished at 4 o'clock, I would have a little evening time to make my dream come true.

That night, as I drifted to sleep I could see a nice cutthroat trout jumping completely out of the water. I had just shut my eyes, or so I thought, when some trumpet player started playing reveille at triple forte, which meant he was way louder than he should be! I got up, looking for something to throw, and then noticed all the light coming into the window. I looked at the clock. It was 6:03 AM! Didn't these people know it was summer? Summer meant sleeping in, at least in previous years it did.

"How'd ya sleep?"

The question came from Ray, one of the teachers staying in my cabin.

"Sleep? What sleep?"

Ray laughed. "Well, at least the chow is pretty good. I'll see ya down at the Mess."

As I strolled to the big building, I saw the trumpet player heading back to his cabin.

"You don't happen to own any mutes, do you?" I asked, hopefully. He just continued on, laughing.

I continued to the Mess Hall and noticed all of the kids were there. "They sure are quieter in the morning, aren't they?" I thought.

"Well, aren't they?" It was Priscilla.

"What?"

"I commented that the boys and girls are quieter in the morning. Probably still waking up," she responded.

"I like it," I replied.

Priscilla pointed and said, "The buffet line is over there. I need to get back to the kitchen." As she headed that way she said, with a smile, "See you at band class!"

I meandered to the buffet table and fixed myself a plate of eggs and pancakes. Unlike Mabel's Café, the pancakes actually looked like pancakes. The coffee was good and the other teachers were very nice, and interesting, too. Ray told of some of his experiences in the Marines. He also told of a beautiful trout stream only half of a mile away, east of here. "The trout are the most plentiful I've ever seen," he remarked. That led to fish stories all around the table. If you've ever been in a group of adults telling fish stories, then you know that not only do the stories grow but the fish do, too.

Near the end of breakfast Ray said, "I'll be taking some kids for a little hike just before lunch and any teachers or counselors are invited. How about you, Greg?"

Thinking that I might get a chance to see that beautiful stream from my daydream I said, "Sure."

At the end of breakfast everybody headed to the class for which they were signed up. I taught the morning band & guitar classes, and then met up with Ray and about 8 kids.

"Hello, Mr. Olson," said one smiling youngster. "We're the Sea Snakes and my name is Charley!"

"How nice," I replied, hoping that the Sea Snakes would be heading for water.

Ray took the lead, with me in the rear. He led us on a well-maintained trail through the woods at a fairly brisk pace. It had just dawned on me that Ray used to be a Marine, and looked like he was still in pretty good shape.

"When do you think we'll get to the stream?" I puffed.

Charley responded, "We won't be going to any stream today, Mr. Olson. We're going up there!" Charley pointed to a crest that was difficult to make out because of the clouds that were below it.

"We're going up there?" I choked.

"Yep."

"But I don't see a trail!"

"It's hidden behind those huge boulders that we have to climb," he stated. "I took this same hike last year."

"And you survived?" I gasped, rhetorically.

We did an elevation gain of about 800 feet and paused to rest in a clump of trees.

Happy to have survived the hard part of the trail I wheezed, "I'm glad that's over!"

Ray announced, "All right, people. We're going to take a little rest here before we do the hard part."

"Why are your eyes so big, Mr. Olson?" asked Charley.

"Oh, I'm just trying to let in more light so that I can see the crest." Looking towards the direction we were last headed, I wheezed," I can't seem to make it out."

"That's because you're looking the wrong direction, Mr. Olson. It's that way."

Charley was holding his index finger straight up. I kept waiting for him to point north, south, east or west but his finger remained at the straight-up direction. As I looked up, I saw what looked to be a trail chiseled out of the granite.

"Maybe we'll see a mountain goat up there, Mr. Olson!"

"They're too smart to go up something that steep!" I choked. "Have they ever thought of putting a rope tow or elevator in this section?"

"Oh, Mr. Olson. You're such a kidder!"

I thought, "Why do these people think I'm kidding?"

I won't bore you with the details of the climb, which Ray called a little hike, other than to say I made it to the top and survived.

At the top Charley said, "Why are you on your hands and knees, Mr. Olson?"

"I'm just…(wheeze)…trying to find….(pant)….a rare form of….(wheeze)…lichen that only grows where…..(gurgle)….there's no oxygen."

"OK, kids. We only get 10 minutes here and then we have to head back down," came the announcement from Ray, who was NOT breathing hard and, in fact, wasn't even perspiring!"

"What?" I gasped. "This is so beautiful. Shouldn't we enjoy this view a little longer?"

"Mr. Olson," responded Charley, "these clouds have covered the mountain top. You can't see a thing!"

I was beginning to see why Charley was included with the Sea Snakes, which are considered some of the most poisonous snakes on the planet.

"All right, let's go!" shouted Ray.

As I scrambled to my feet, Charley helped me stabilize myself.

"But I LIKE clouds," I said.

That evening I was asleep before my head hit the pillow. And here I was again, with hundreds of cutthroat trout leaping over boulders in the middle of that beautiful stream. And, just as suddenly, a goose flew right by my head, honking in my ear. My eyes flew open in time for me to hear the last strains of reveille by an extremely loud trumpet. As I got up I noticed Ray was already gone. I headed to breakfast and I saw Priscilla putting a pitcher of orange juice on a table.

"How'd you sleep?" she inquired.

"Remind me to fill that trumpet player's mouthpiece with epoxy," I grumbled.

Priscilla smiled. "Oh, Mr. Olson….."

"I know….I'm such a kidder!" I said without smiling.

The rest of the day was uneventful except for using up most of the Infirmary's band-aids for my feet.

The next day, however, became the most exciting day of the camp. It all had to do with that dream of the pristine trout stream. You see, during the lunch period I took a little walk around the lake to find the outgoing stream. Unfortunately, I discovered that the stream went right along the forbidden path. Rats! I just HAD to get to Ray's trout stream.

After my classes that day I took a stroll over to the east side of the lake. Usually on a stroll I don't have a fly pole and a creel, but I was a determined man. When I got to the east side of the lake, there were the red ribbons around various trees just like Pete said. There was also a sign there. It read, "PROCEED NO FURTHER!" Just below that sentence was a skull and crossbones. Below that was, "BEWARE OF BEAR WITH CUBS." And below that in smaller print, "IF YOU PROCEED BEYOND THIS POINT YOU ARE TAKING YOUR LIFE INTO YOUR OWN HANDS". Below that someone had scratched, YUM YUM.

To show the power that a fish has over a fisherman, even with all of those warnings, I was already rationalizing:

"I'll bet that Pete made up that story to keep the stream to himself! He was afraid it would get fished out!"

and, "If there was a bear, she would be with her cubs where all the huckleberries are on the other side of the mountain."

and, "I'll just make a lot of noise so she'll hear me coming."

So, you can see that rationality can sometimes go out the window when it comes to fishing. As I meandered down the path I listened intently for any noises. After continuing a while and becoming a little more nervous, I started whistling so that my sounds would scare the bear (if there was one) away. I made it all the way to the stream without any sign of bear. "Aha," I thought. "Pete WAS just keeping this to himself!"

The stream was even more pristine and beautiful than in my dreams. The fish weren't jumping in the hundreds, but there definitely were cutthroat in this stream, as was proven in the next hour. It was a thoroughly enjoyable experience, with me limiting out within 45 minutes. What a great day!

I should amend that statement to read: What a great day until that moment. I heard the bellow before I saw her. There, on the other side of the stream, about 300 hundred yards upstream, was Momma Bear, with two little cubs beside her. I used to think black bears were not that big. I decided that since I had just limited out it might be time to go. The biggest problem was that Momma Bear was between the trail and me. I decided to go down the hill a little ways and then cut back around to catch the trail behind her.

I slowly backed into the forest behind me, keeping an eye on Momma Bear. She didn't move yet, other than to stand on her hind legs and bellow. As I lost sight of her, I picked my way down the hill the best I could. The underbrush wasn't totally thick, yet there was plenty of it. I decided at this point that I might just run a little ways. That decision was prompted by the fact that I felt I should be trying to get in better shape while I'm out here in the wilds. The crashing behind me also might have helped in that decision.

As I raced down the hill, I thought that the fish smell was probably driving Momma Bear on, and that she felt the need to feed her cubs. Trying to be agreeable and knowing that Cutthroat probably tasted better than human, I dropped my creel and kept running. I figured the crashing sounds behind me might stop any moment. Sure enough, after about another minute they had stopped. I paused to catch my breath while listening. It seemed that Momma Bear was happy with her free dinner. As I was beginning to think where to make my turn for my cutback, the crashing sound started again and was getting louder. Leaving my pole right there I ran downhill, crashing through brush, ripping my pants, scratching arms and face, and thinking maybe Pete was on the level about the bear.

All of a sudden, I came out onto a logging road and there, standing next to a car, was another fisherman.

"Quick!" I yelled. "I'm being chased by a bear! You've got to get us out of here!"

As he stood there and didn't move I noticed he was an Asian-looking man. I also noticed that he didn't understand a thing I said. As I ran towards him I made signs of what I thought a hungry bear looked like. What he saw was a wild man, running at him, growling and waving his arms. The Asian's eyes grew huge as he leapt into his car and started the motor.

"Great!" I thought. "He understood!" As I reached the passenger side of the car he took off, throwing gravel and dirt everywhere.

"Wait!" I screamed, while chasing after the car. "Come back!"

As I ran, I turned to see the bear crashing out of the forest, making a beeline right for me!

"Stop!" I yelled.

I'm not sure if he understood, or saw that bear in his rearview mirror, but he slammed on his brakes causing me to crash right into his trunk - knocking the breath out of me. He then helped me into the passenger side, dazed as I was, and ran to the driver side. Before he could peel out, there was a huge "Whump!" from the back of the car and we were propelled forward. As the car sped away, there was the bear right behind us.

The road curved left and started going uphill. This is where I found out how stupid black bears were. Instead of following the road, she bounded to her left into the brush where the traveling MUST be more difficult. "Whump!" came the crash to the left side of the Asian's car, barely missing his driver's side window!

"Yeow!" yelled the Asian.

"Yeow!" yelled the band teacher.

"Roar!" yelled Momma Bear.

As we headed up the mountain, I could see Momma Bear chasing and then slowing, and falling way behind.

"I think she gave up!" I yelled to the driver. All I got back was a wide-eyed stare as he raced on. I noticed that we were getting close to the crest of the ridge where the road took a hairpin before the lake.

Realizing how close we were to that hairpin I shouted, "You better slow down!" He just looked wild-eyed and continued on at 50 miles-per-hour.

The turn was rapidly approaching so I used my best Asian and said, "You slow car now, OK?" while using hand motions to indicate slowing. I must have been using the wrong dialect, because fifty feet from the hairpin he sped up, shooting us over the guardrail and about 30 feet into the lake. As we scrambled out the windows, the Asian began to talk. By the volume and pitch of his voice, and how fast he was screaming his words, I had a feeling he was not saying, "I'm so glad you're safe now. Don't worry about my car and can I get you anything?"

I swam a little faster. He swam a little faster. I swam to my left. He swam to his left. I swam to my right. He swam to his right. I got out of the water and started running towards the parking lot. He was right on my tail. I ran into the woods and he followed me. I came out by my cabin and saw Priscilla.

"Mr. Olson, we missed you at dinner!" she exclaimed.

As I raced past her, heading towards my car, I asked, "What did you have?"

"Cutthroat Trout!" was her reply.

Greg
Metcalf
makes
his
ABOUT THE AUTHOR   home
in
wonderful
Washington
State and
has
taught
music for
over
three
decades.
Even
though he
believes
in adding
a "touch
of humor"
to his
lessons,
he has always held
the bar high while encouraging his
students to achieve success in all of their
learning. Greg loves the mountains and
forests of Washington and tends to find
himself with a backpack and/or fishing rod
as he meanders on some backwoods trail.
That is, when he is not performing in
some show or jazz club
in Seattle.

11183471R00098

Made in the USA
Charleston, SC
05 February 2012